✱ how to make quick & easy cards ✱

Paper
Simply Paper

✱ Lesley Ballantine

Published in Australia by Lesley Ballantine 2012

© Lesley Ballantine 2012

Design, layout and photography by Carrie Green.

Except as provided by the *Copyright Act 1968*, no part of this publication may be reproduced, stored in a retrieval system or transmitted in any form or by any means, without the prior written permission of the publisher.

National Library of Australia Cataloguing-in-Publication entry.

Author: Lesley Ballantine

Title: Paper Simply Paper

ISBN 978-0-9873354-2-5

Subjects – Greeting cards. Paper work.

Dewey number: 745.5941

DISCLAIMER: The information in this book is presented in good faith. All care has been taken in writing of instructions and drawing of diagrams but no warranty is given nor results guaranteed. All effort has been made to comply with copyright.

Photocopies or printing of designs, templates or diagrams can be made only for personal use.

All materials and tools available from major craft stores.

All measurements are in metric units (millimetres) and standard international paper sizes.

Difficulty Ratings

✽	Cards are 'quick and easy'
✽✽	A little bit fiddly
✽✽✽	May take a bit of time on your first attempt
✽✽✽✽	Yes, these take time but are well worth the effort!

My sincere thanks to:

My daughter Rayna for urging me to commit my cards to this book.

My husband Ean for his ever-obliging assistance building display stands, packing up for shows, fixing props and his patience living with a paper trail through the house for over ten years now.

Carrie for her assistance during the shows and her design and photography for the book.

Val, Ellen, Penny, Jacky and Maureen for sharing their ideas over the past several years.

Murray for hosting my websites and for all his technical assistance.

Theo and Marga for exciting products and wonderful workshops.

All my customers who encouraged me at the shows with their enthusiasm for my style of cards.

Dedicated to my crafty granddaughter Kyela

Contents

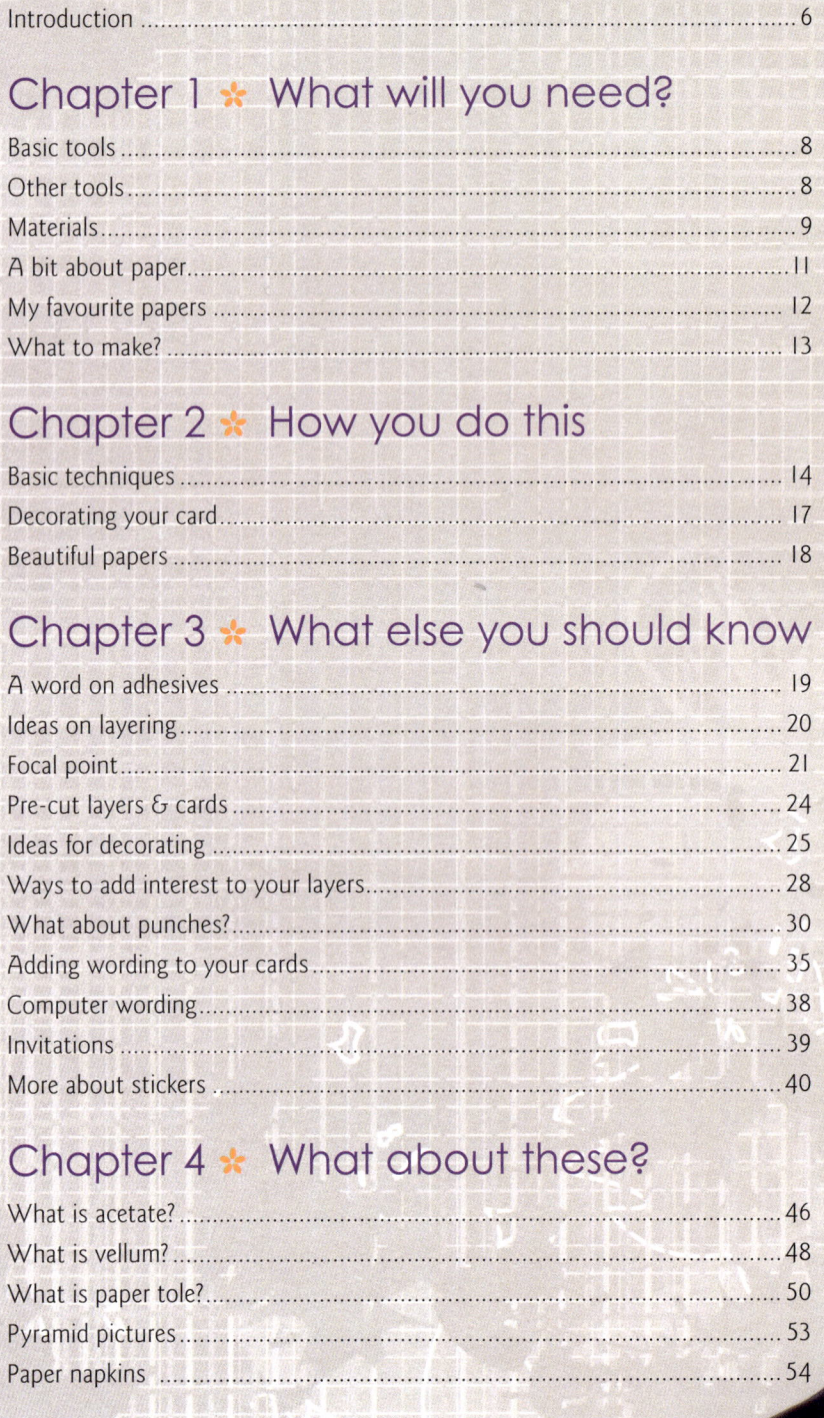

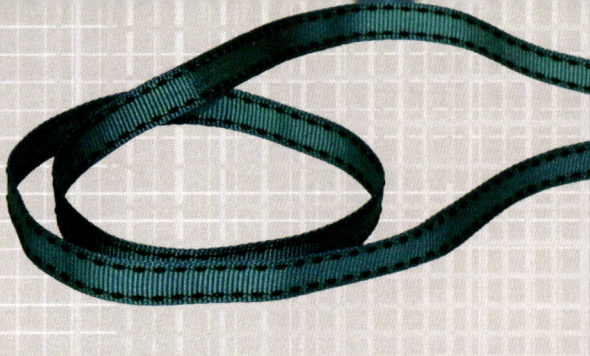

Introduction 6

Chapter 1 ✻ What will you need?
Basic tools 8
Other tools 8
Materials 9
A bit about paper 11
My favourite papers 12
What to make? 13

Chapter 2 ✻ How you do this
Basic techniques 14
Decorating your card 17
Beautiful papers 18

Chapter 3 ✻ What else you should know
A word on adhesives 19
Ideas on layering 20
Focal point 21
Pre-cut layers & cards 24
Ideas for decorating 25
Ways to add interest to your layers 28
What about punches? 30
Adding wording to your cards 35
Computer wording 38
Invitations 39
More about stickers 40

Chapter 4 ✻ What about these?
What is acetate? 46
What is vellum? 48
What is paper tole? 50
Pyramid pictures 53
Paper napkins 54

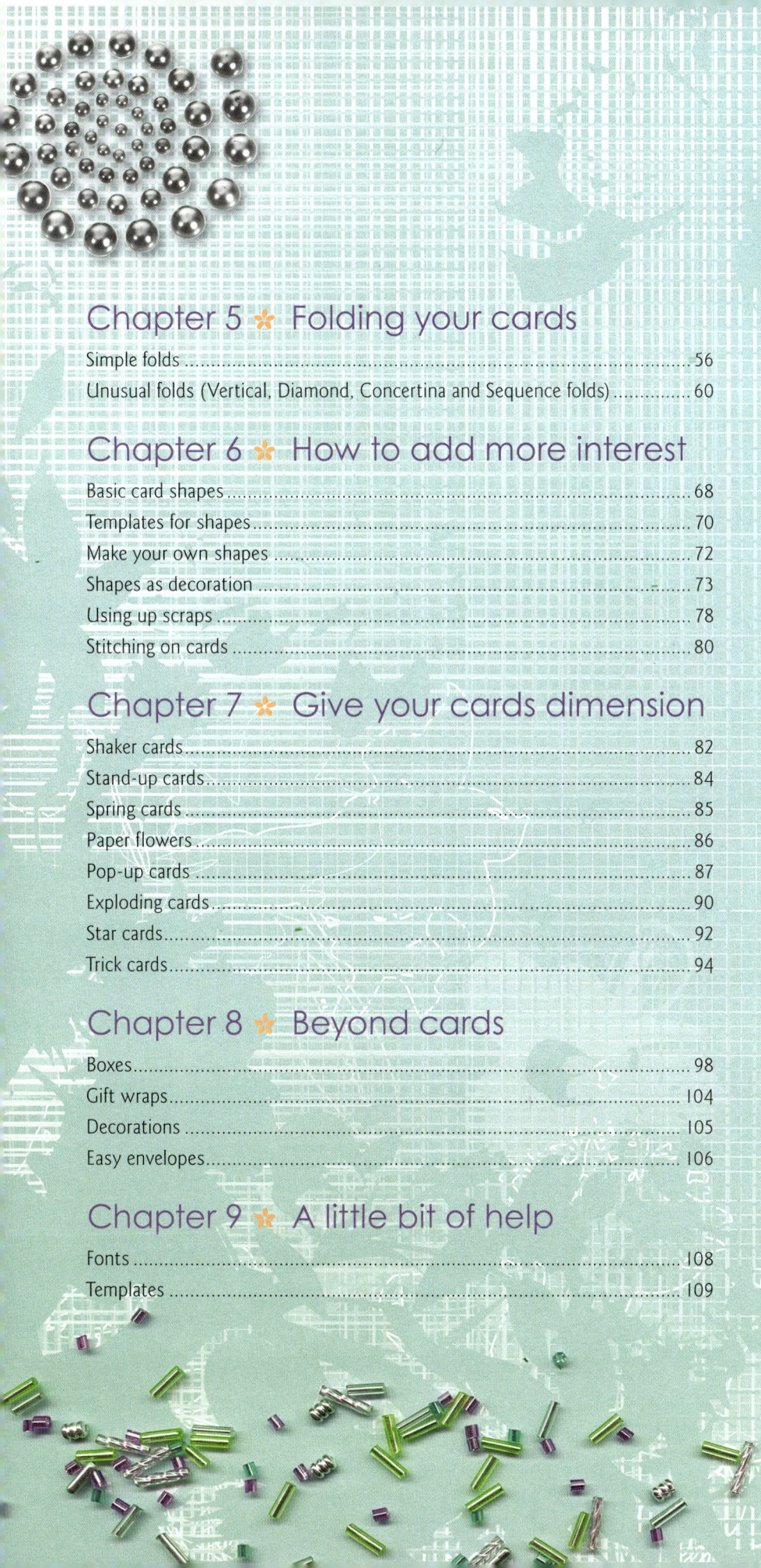

Chapter 5 ✽ Folding your cards
Simple folds 56
Unusual folds (Vertical, Diamond, Concertina and Sequence folds) 60

Chapter 6 ✽ How to add more interest
Basic card shapes 68
Templates for shapes 70
Make your own shapes 72
Shapes as decoration 73
Using up scraps 78
Stitching on cards 80

Chapter 7 ✽ Give your cards dimension
Shaker cards 82
Stand-up cards 84
Spring cards 85
Paper flowers 86
Pop-up cards 87
Exploding cards 90
Star cards 92
Trick cards 94

Chapter 8 ✽ Beyond cards
Boxes 98
Gift wraps 104
Decorations 105
Easy envelopes 106

Chapter 9 ✽ A little bit of help
Fonts 108
Templates 109

Introduction

Welcome to my book. My aim is to share my years of card making with a picture book full of ideas.

I have run my own paper craft business for over ten years. I sold online as Paper Dazee and exhibited at craft fairs on Australia's east coast. During the years of displaying my cards on the craft show circuit, people were forever asking how I made my cards and could they take photos.

Finally, now in my retirement, I am proud to put together a selection of my cards and some basic tips and techniques to help you all create quick and easy cards. I am not a scrapbooker, though a lot of what I do could easily carry over to scrapbooking. Nor am I a stamper. I simply let the papers do the work.

I use very basic tools, a few punches and an assortment of accessories for decoration. My aim is to keep it simple.

Despite our world of technology, I believe that most people still enjoy receiving a card with a hand written message inside. If that card has been made especially for them, it is even more meaningful. There are so many occasions that can be acknowledged with a card so someone knows you are thinking of them.

Though I touch on a lot of subjects in the book, I am sharing with you the things that I have found I use over and over, mainly as they are quick, easy, economical and readily available.

People make cards for many and varied reasons. To be creative, to add that personal touch, to make exactly what they want, to save money, for a pleasant pastime or hobby or to sell for extra income.

For whatever occasion and whatever your objective, I hope you find enjoyment in the following pages, pick up some valuable tips and techniques and can hold me responsible for sending you on a wonderful journey into the world of

Paper, Simply, Paper.

Lesley Ballantine

WARNING! Collecting beautiful papers can be addictive. I ended up with a whole store!

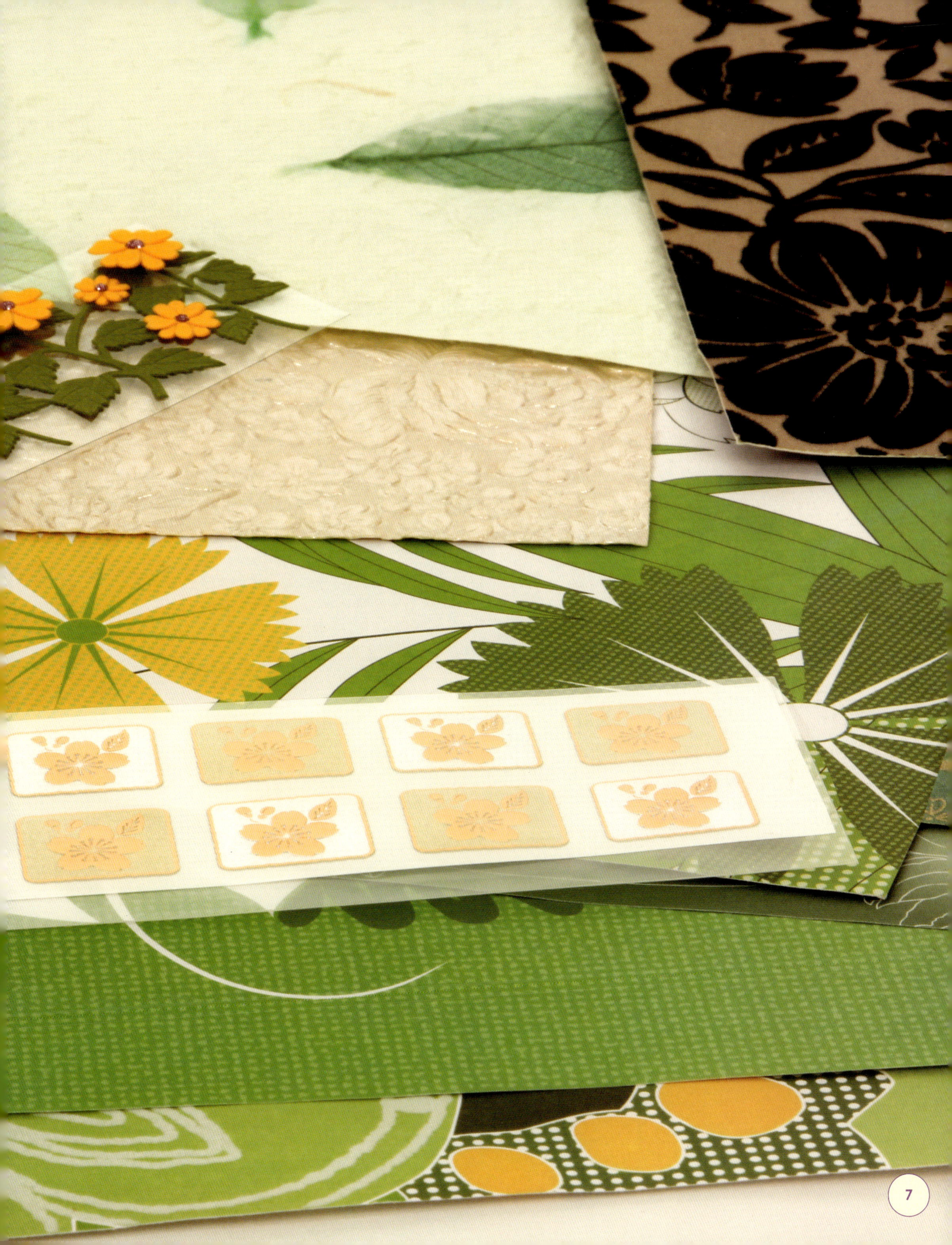

Chapter 1 ✻ What will you need?

Basic tools

You can start making your own cards with very basic tools.

Mat

You need to work on a firm smooth surface. Craft mats are self-healing when cut by a knife and are readily available from craft suppliers. They vary in price but I have found that the inexpensive ones from the dollar shops are as good as any. I do all my measuring on my mat, so I prefer the whole mat marked in a 10mm grid, (or similar if using imperial measure).

Knife

Despite all the craft knives on the market, I do most of my base cutting with a utility knife from any hardware store. They are inexpensive, tough and replacement blades are easy to get anywhere. I like the control I get from using these chunky knives.

Ruler

You will need a metal ruler or your knife will soon have a plastic or timber one shredded. Again, usually found at any hardware store. 450mm is good length.

Scissors

I do all my straight cutting with my knife on my mat. I only use my scissors for cutting out fiddly pictures. Mine are small with a fine tip and if you can find scissors with non-stick blades that is a big advantage if you do a lot of your work with double sided tape as I do.

Pencil

I rarely measure any card with a ruler. I judge sizing by eye and use a tiny pencil mark for my cutting line, then square it on the grid on my mat.

Scoring tool

Scoring is the process of running a groove in your card along a fold line. You can improvise with a blunt knife but I use a bone scorer. **This would be my favourite tool.** A genuine bone scorer never wears out, does not leave marks on your work and has some flex in it. Once you have folded your card run the bone scorer along the spine to give a sharp professional finish. See page 14.

Other tools

These items are very handy though not essential.

Pricking tool

This basically is a needle with a handle. Very handy for picking up fiddly bits. I particularly like it when applying adhesive foam squares to my papers or peeling stickers off a sheet.

Tweezers

Pointed nose tweezers work best.

Circle cutter

A simple one is all you need. Mine is like a set of compasses with a blade in one arm and a point in the other.

8

Removable tape

This is sticky but can be pulled off with no damage to your papers. It is available at newsagents and can also be called "Invisible Tape".

Trimmer

There are many trimmers on the market. Identify just what your needs are before you invest in one. I mostly use mine to cut my stock to standard sizes.

A note on electronic tools

There is now a whole world of computer programs and electronic tools which design, cut and emboss and that is just the start. You can produce your own beautiful papers and decorative items to utilise in many of my cards using these tools but this book does not address their use specifically.

Materials

Cardstock

I prefer a fairly thick cardstock for my base card. 250gsm is ideal. A4 (297x210mm) is a practical size and scrapbook 12x12's (300x300mm) are also useful. White, cream and black are always a good standby. See page 11 for more on paper sizes.

Decorative papers

You will need a good assortment of papers of all colours, textures and patterns to add to your cards. Whenever you see a nice piece, just add it to your stash. 12x12 prints are excellent. Especially sets or double sided sheets that coordinate with each other.

Writing papers

It is nice to add a sheet of paper inside your card for a personal message. Most office suppliers will have A4 sheets. White or cream is a good start, though coloured papers can be useful for layering.

Envelopes

Unless you want to be making your own envelopes, ALWAYS make your card to fit the size envelope that is available. I make my cards to fit the three main size envelopes available in Australia. C6 (162x114.5mm) DL (110x220mm) and Square (150mm). Wedding stationers or newsagents are the best places to find these. White and cream are always useful.

Adhesives

My preference is double sided tape 6mm wide. It is dry, so does not warp your paper and is very easy to use. I also have a fine tipped glue pen for fiddly bits and PVA glue for adding any solid item such as a button. At times I may use a glue stick, readily available from newsagents.

Decorative items

Yes. **You certainly need some bling!** Collect your choice of decorative items and include sparkle and shine if this is your style.

Like all crafts, there is no end to the tools, papers and accessories on the market. The joy of card making is that you do not need to outlay a fortune to start and you can build up as you go. Later in this book I will point out a few more of my favourite tools and give many tips to help you on your journey.

Envelopes can come in many shapes and sizes, however check the postage costs before you choose non-standard sizes

A bit about paper

Weight of paper and card stock

All paper and card is measured by the amount of paper pulp it has per square metre. The term is gsm (grams per square metre). The more pulp, the thicker the sheet and the higher the gsm. Most paper packaging will indicate the gsm. As a guide:

20gsm is tissue paper.

80gsm is copy paper.

90-120gsm is good quality writing 'text' stock. Ideal for inserts and decorating card fronts.

130-190gsm is lightweight card. Good for punching or layering but too flimsy for actual cards.

200-300 gsm. Good for card making. My ideal is 250gsm.

Over 300gsm is becoming cardboard weight. These will crack when you try to fold them.

Sizes of paper and cardstock

Paper and card are produced in very large mill sheets available at specialty paper stores. However most papers are cut to standard sizes for printers and photocopiers. A4 (297x210mm) is the standard size used in Australia.

Simply cut an A4 in half to A5 (210x148mm) and this is a perfect size for cards. When this A5 is folded in half it will fit the standard C6 (162x114mm) envelopes on the market. Stores that sell wedding stationery will carry good quality card stock, papers and envelopes in these sizes.

Another useful and readily available size is the 12x12. Actually 12 inches square or 300x300mm. These are scrapbooking papers available from all scrapbook suppliers. Cut these in half to make your square cards. Trim them down by a few mm to fit your square envelopes. Most square envelopes will be 150mm or 160mm square.

How boring I hear some of you say. I want to make all different size cards!

Of course you can make a card ANY SIZE YOU WANT. There are NO RULES. But you will then have to track down envelopes to suit or make your own. Some sizes attract extra cost in postage. This could be significant if you are making a large number of wedding invitations to send far and wide.

NOTE: Refer to this page for actual sizes used throughout this book.

Standard paper sizes

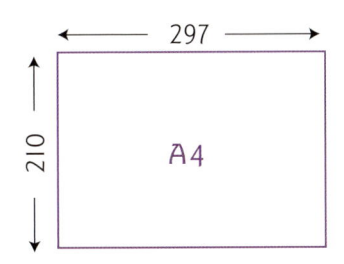

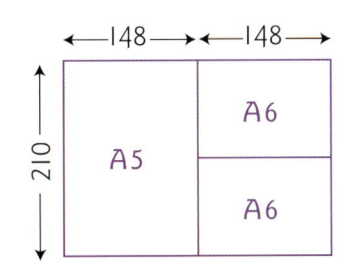

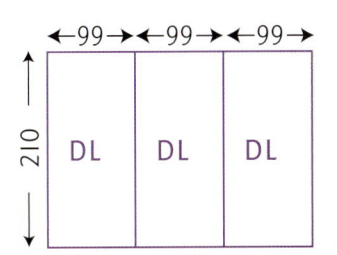

A4 — 297 x 210

A5 — 148 x 210, A6 — 148 x (half of 210)

DL — 99 x 210 (three across)

Most common envelope sizes

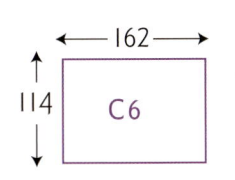

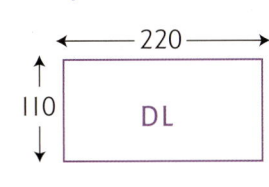

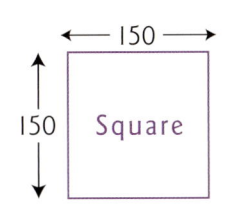

C6 — 162 x 114

DL — 220 x 110

Square — 150 x 150

11

My favorite papers

Metallics

120gsm text or 250-280gsm card. Available at most wedding stationers. These look impressive and have the same colour on both sides. The text is lovely for layering and great to punch. Many have beautiful prints on them. They are excellent to print on with your inkjet printer. You should also find envelopes to match in C6, square and DL business size.

Japanese papers

I love Japanese prints and the gorgeous silk of mulberry papers. Very beautiful handmade papers are now available from many oriental regions. I collect any papers with an interesting texture or design just like a patchworker collects fabrics. I may have no special need for it right away. It is just added to the stash.

Scrapbook papers

Scrapbook papers can be very useful printed stock. Especially double-sided papers if each side complements the other. Many brands have sets of papers. This gives you a wide selection of papers that you know will easily coordinate with each other for some stunning effects.

NOTE: A beautiful piece of paper is often all you need to decorate a card. Sometimes they may seem expensive but the more ornate, the smaller the piece you need to be effective. See page 18.

There are web sites with papers and collage pictures available for download often for free. Just search for 'downloadable papers for cardmaking'

What to make?

"Where do you get your ideas?" people always ask me.

I don't just have ideas in my head. I let them evolve once I am inspired by something I have seen elsewhere.

Maybe another card I have received, magazines and books, craft fairs, craft stores or on the net.

Once I have a basic plan, my own style develops as the card progresses.

Ask yourself…

Who is this card for? What is the occasion? What size card do I want to make? Do I have a colour scheme in mind or a specific item I wish to use? How long have I got to make this card? Will it be 'quick and easy' or a masterpiece?

What next?

Once you have an idea in mind, select one main item that you want to use. It might be a certain piece of paper or a particular item to add to the card front. Take note of the main colours in this item. Now go to your paper stash and pull out a few prints and plain pieces that have these colours predominantly. Don't have anything specific in mind. You will find that a combination of papers quite unexpected will suddenly have the WOW factor. Once you have selected the pieces you could utilise, select a cardstock that will set it off best.

Where did this paper stash come from?

I am not going to tell you exactly where to buy the papers I use or the items I add as decoration. My aim is to inspire you to embark on a journey accumulating papers of all types, colour, texture and weight plus items from far and wide for your decorations. You never know when these items will be just exactly what you need.

What colours go well together?

If you are unsure what colours to combine, a colour wheel is very useful. These are inexpensive and readily available from art supply stores. One side should have the base colours with their shades and tones and diagonally opposite their complimentary colours. From the wheel below red should work best with green but blues to yellows are worth considering. What are the traditional colours of Christmas?

Chapter 2 ✶ How you do this

Basic techniques

Cutting your cardstock

Put a pencil mark where you want to cut your cardstock.

On your mat line up one straight edge of your card on a horizontal grid line and the pencil mark on a vertical grid line.

Using your ruler and knife cut down the vertical line towards yourself. Hold the ruler firm. Several light cuts are better than one heavy cut, as your ruler can easily move.

Folding your cardstock

Put a pencil mark where you want to fold your cardstock. Line up as above and score down the vertical grid line.

Fold your card on the score line.

Run your tool along the edge of the paper to get a sharp fold.

> **TIP**
> Always keep your knife blade very sharp so you can use lighter pressure on the blade. This reduces chance of slipping or dragging the paper edge.

Trimming and squaring your card

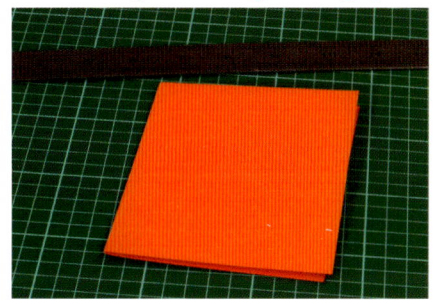

Often when you fold your card it may not overlap exactly or may not fit easily into your envelope.

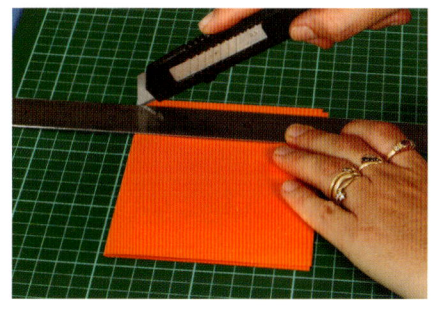

This is quickly rectified by trimming the uneven edges with your knife. Line up your folded edge on a grid line and trim.

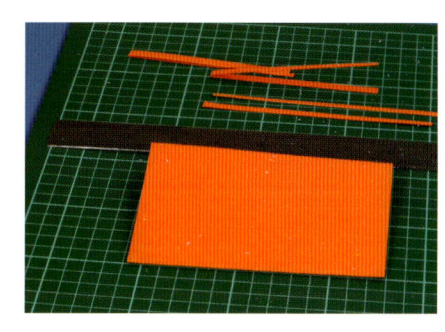

Remember to use the grid lines on your mat to keep it square.

Adding an insert

Fold your text paper in half. There is no need to score text weight papers.

Place it in your card just where you want it to sit. Pencil mark your cutting lines and trim.

Add a piece of double-sided tape on the front just next to the fold.

Put it back in your card exactly where you want it keeping borders equal. Peel off the tape and close your card pressing down on the tape.

This way the insert is attached to the front of your card. It will open when you open the card. It also leaves the back of the card free from the insert which is good if you want to sell your cards and slip the envelope in the back.

Ideas for inserts
- You can leave inserts out, but they give your card a more professional look.
- You can use a single sheet, a folded sheet or multiple layers which work well for wedding invitations to include accommodation details, gift register info and RSVP requirements.
- You can print a message on an insert using your computer before you fold and trim it.
- You can scan a message from an old card and print it on your insert.

Adding a simple layer

If you put your picture onto another layer of paper or card of a complementary colour, it will give the picture more highlight.

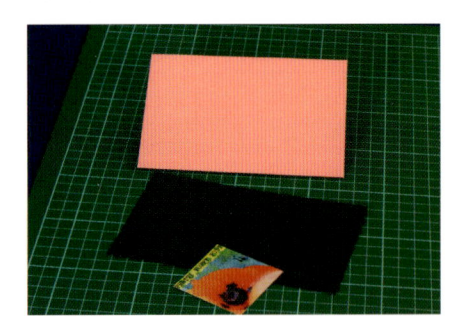

Select your picture and choose a complementary colour background.

Make sure your picture and your background layer have straight sides and square corners before you start. Trim if need be.

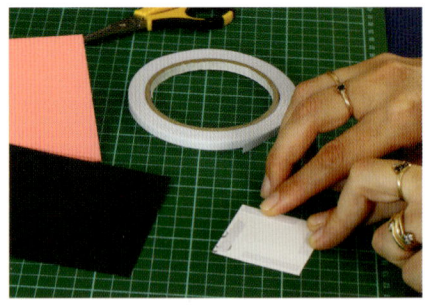

I use 6mm double sided tape for all my layers and large pictures. It is quick, clean and dry unlike glues which can warp your paper.

I don't put tape all the way around the layer, nor precisely on the edge. I put four pieces starting in each corner. I add extra on long sides if necessary.

Make sure all corners are secure.

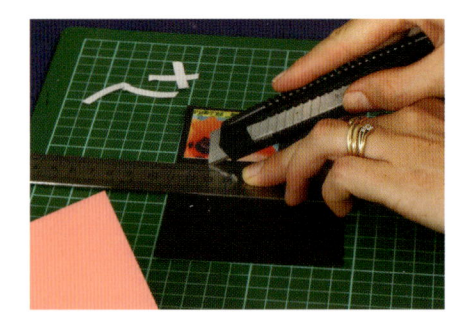

Adhere your picture to your layer leaving the desired width of edge on the top and one side. Pencil mark your cutting lines on the remaining sides and trim using the grid on your mat.

Now select your main card stock to complement the picture and adhere this combined picture and layer to the card front.

NOTE: To add a background directly to your card, sit the background in the top left hand corner of your card in as far as you want from the corner. Pencil mark the cutting lines for the other side and the bottom, then line up on your mat and trim to fit. For example, in Card 3 the picture and wording have a red layer under them. The card itself has a double background.

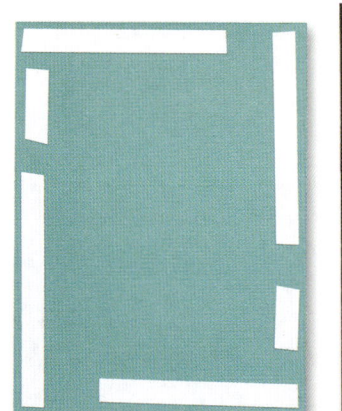

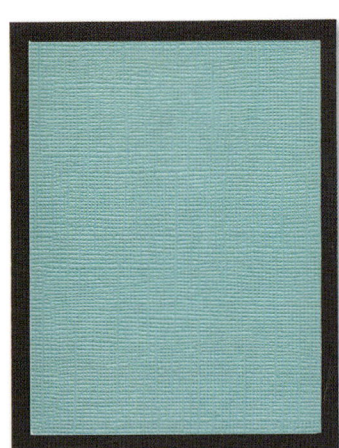

Decorating your card

Recycling old cards
This can be as simple or as involved as you want to make it. The easiest of all is to utilise old cards by cutting the fronts off and often the writing as well.

Card 1 Leaves
This picture was from an old card. I have put it on a white layer, punched two holes and tied with coloured twine.

Card 2 Snowmen
The red in the picture is accentuated by the red layer behind. The wording in this card was also cut from the original card, put on a red layer and mounted on foam. See page 19 for foam mount.

Card 3 Val's Christmas
A beautiful background layer adds a totally new look to an old card. **Thank you Val.**

Card 4 Christmas trees
You can cut your picture and spread it over the layer for more interest.

Card 5 Flower vase
Here I have cut the card on the diagonal.

Card 6 Candles
You can be as inventive as you wish with this cutting and can also add more layers.

"Using old cards to decorate new ones is a quick and easy method"

17

Beautiful papers

Decorating a card front with beautiful paper is often all that is required.

Card 7 Yellow flowers ✿
This is simply a print from a scrapbook 12x12 sheet. I have added a few pearls and a trinket plus a sticker message. Nothing more.

Card 8 Pink blossom ✿
The pink blossoms are also from a 12x12 sheet and I have added a background layer. Note the trim added to the envelope as well.

Card 9 Simplicity ✿
Butting two pieces of paper that complement each other is also effective. I have covered the join between the two papers with a strip of ribbon.

Card 10 Come home soon ✿
Mini pictures can also be combined to give a simple card. These travel stamps can seem as one with a single background.

Card 11 Postcards from where? ✿
Here each picture has its own individual layer plus an overall background layer.

Chapter 3 ✻ What else you should know

A word on adhesives

Double-sided tapes
These come in varying widths and can also be bought by the sheet. Full sheets are useful if you have a large number of cards to make as it is less fiddly.

Glue pens
These work well for fiddly pieces of paper and come in varying tip sizes with both repositionable and permanent glues.

PVA glue
I use PVA glue for solid items such as buttons. It takes about 30 minutes to set but once dry it is fixed tight and dries clear.

Foam mount
If you prefer your work to have a raised three dimensional effect, use double sided mounting foam. Mounting foam is available as flat sheets, rolls, cut into strips, squares and circles including very tiny pieces. The thickness can also vary. For most card making 1-2mm thick is quite adequate. See the wording in card 9.
It is raised using the foam mount.

19

Ideas on layering

Card 12 Peace dove ✳
You can build up layers any way you wish and offset them rather than evenly stacked one on top of the other. Many layers have been used to fill this square card front. The small picture is from a recycled card.

Card 13 Friends ✳
The central leaves are a sticker and the layers are offset to add more interest.

Card 14 Lovely lady ✳
I have taken my colours from the picture. The pink layer has a scalloped edge using a border punch. See page 30.

Card 15 Thank You Flower ✳✳
You can alternate the colours of your layers. I took my colours from those in the flower.

- My cardstock is 260x130mm, scored and folded to a 130mm square.
- The main layer is 120mm square. The green is 120x80mm and the pink 120x40mm joined together with removable tape.
- The smaller layer is 80x80 mm. The pink is 80x60mm and the green 80x20mm joined together.
- The top cream layer is 70x70mm.

Card 16 Butterfly ✳✳
This actually starts out as a circular layer.

- My cardstock is 260x130mm, scored and folded to an 130mm square.
- The green dot layer is 125x125mm.
- For the top layer cut a circle radius 55mm. Total circle diameter 110mm.
- Cut this circle into four quarters.
- Arrange your four quarters on your background layer. I have used bendable border stickers to accent the edges. See page 42 for border stickers.
- The central butterfly is a sticker.

Focal point

Dividing the card into sections can direct the eye to a focal point. Using this technique you need less of your decorative paper and can use a smaller item on your card as your main decoration.

Dividing the card front in half

This is my favourite quick card.

Card 17 Olive branch ✽

- I used a strip of decorative paper half the width of my card front.
- I cut the dove from a 12x12 sheet.
- I adhered it onto a square with 2 actual layers.
- I have used tiny sticker dots to highlight the centre line.

Note how the dove extends off the square layer.

Card 18 Belle fleur ✽

A stunning glitter paper and a flower is all I used with a border sticker in the centre. Glitter paper would be found in a specialty paper store.

Card 19 Buttons ✽

I cut out the little picture and mounted it with foam on several layers. I added a half layer in coordinating colours and a couple of real buttons to define the centre.

Card 20 Butterflies in silhouette ✽

The butterflies are a sticker. One sticker is all you need plus a message to fill a card front using this divide technique.

Card 21 Lady in waiting ✽

Decorate your card front horizontally using the same divide technique. The lady is a very tiny picture, yet is still enough when layered and given a beautiful background. I have used a textured paper and added pearls.

Tip

Decorate the "heart". All the tall cards on this page have their focal point about one third down the card, similar to where to human heart sits.

21

Focal point
(continued)

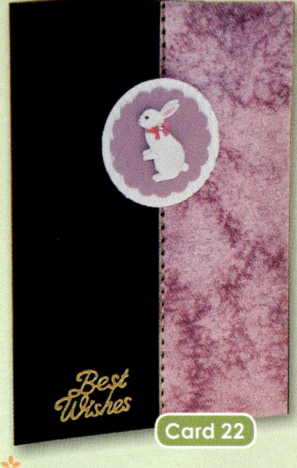

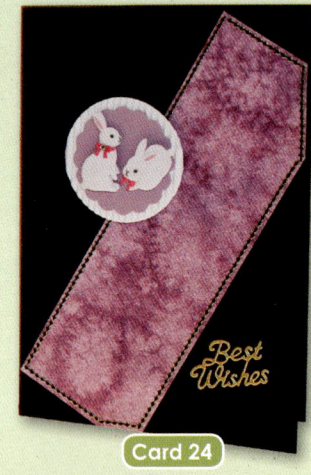

Cards 22-24 Rabbits and friend ✿
These three cards are made using the same half strip of pink paper. The rabbits and cat are stickers and I have mounted them on shapes I have punched to make medallions. See page 31 for punching.

Card 25 Going Japanese ✿
Do your divide on the diagonal. An economical use of more expensive papers.

Card 26 Pooh bear ✿
Triangles provide interesting results.

Card 27 Simply happy birthday ✿
This is a cream card. I have cut a wide and a narrow strip of the black and red papers. I have added one of each to each side of the card.

Card 28 **Cherry blossoms** ✿✿

This is a full black layer on a white card with two thin strips of pink paper. A line a rhinestones emphasises the centre. The blossoms were cut from a 12x12 sheet and glued on individually. Some are mounted on foam for a 3D effect and some of the centres have pink pearls in them.

Card 28

Thinking of you

Pre-cut layers & cards

If you want a really quick way to get a focal point, you can often buy pre-cut cards or overlays.

Card 29 Hello ✻

The red layer is a pre-cut overlay with the square cut out. All I now have to concentrate on is decorating that square area. I have chosen here to use my flower punches.

Card 30 Roses are red ✻✻

The background layer to this beautiful paper tole picture is a bought laser cut mat.

Card 31 Lilies ✻✻

This too is a laser cut mat. These are available from specialty paper craft stores but you would have to keep an eye out for them.

Card 32 Miss you ✻

Trifold cards are usually readily available in paper craft stores. They have a window pre cut and a third panel that folds over the back of the window. The windows can be all shapes. All you need to do is decorate using the window as your focal point. The gold edge around this window is part of the card. The urn is a sticker on a specialty paper. I then cut out the entire shape and mounted it on foam. I have decorated the envelope with a paper strip to match.

Card 33 Christmas time ✻

Cut out cards are also often found in paper craft stores. With these the shape is cut out of the front panel and you can see through to the inside of the card. For this double diamond I decorated the two diamond shapes on the front using pictures from old cards but also added a decorative paper to the inside of the card.

Ideas for decorating

Adding something of interest to your cards.

Pictures

Collect these wherever you find them. Sheets in craft stores, old books, old cards, scrapbook pages, die-cut papers, calendars, posters or on the net. Print your own photos or clip art onto paper, vellum or acetate See page 46 acetate and page 48 vellum.

Stickers

The range of product classed as stickers includes pictures, wording, edging, corners, and all kinds of items for scrapbooking. You will find them in grocery stores, dollar shops, newsagents as well as the craft and scrapbook stores. See page 40 for more sticker ideas.

Card 34 Fun and laughter

These pictures were cut from an old card. The two lots of writing are each a rub on. See page 35 for rub ons.

Card 35 Days of olde

These little pictures were on a collage sheet. I have mounted each on black card and joined them with a fine jeweller's wire and a few beads. I used eyelets around the holes I put the wire through but there are stickers that will outline a hole to look like an eyelet. They are much easier to use!

Card 36 Where have they gone?

This lovely picture was on an old poster. I added a tiny scalloped strip to the side and sanded the edge of the picture for an aged look. See page 29 distressing the edge.

Card 37 Fly away

Here I have used split pins to decorate the card. Cut the backs off them and mount them with foam mount.

> **TIP**
>
> **DESIGN PRINCIPLE:** Whatever you add to your cards, odd numbers usually work best. So add one item or three rather than two.
>
> **COST SAVER:** If you have a special picture you want to use more than once, scan it to your computer or photocopy it. Home printers make excellent copies these days. Just check for copyright.

Card 38 Spring is in the air

This is a beautiful background from a 12x12 sheet with a line of daisy stickers.

Ribbons

I use this word loosely. Ginghams, organza, satin, braids, ric rac, felt strips, die-cut satins, meshes, fabric strips and cord. Some can even have wording on them. I use double sided tape to hold ribbons in place. Some craft stores do stock adhesive ribbons which are very easy to use.

Card 39 Flower patch ✿✿

This card has triangular corners of floral paper. Then following the same diagonal line I have alternated different types of ribbon and two rows of pearls. A tiny paper tole picture is then added. See page 50 for paper tole.

Card 40 Miss you dear ✿

This card has a strip of mesh with a die-cut ribbon on top. The background paper complements the colours of the flower.

Card 41 Get well ✿

These papers are from an olde poster. I have inked the edges of the papers. See page 29 inking edges. I have made a ribbon tie from a strip of fabric and frayed the edges.

26

Bling and things!

Bling refers to rhinestones, pearls or anything that sparkles.

Things! Whatever you find. Keep a constant eye out for suitable items to decorate your cards.

Chipboard, wire, die-cut pictures, beads, buttons, tags, jewellery items, buckles, charms, flowers, flowers, flowers…

Card 42 Love ladder ✶
This wire item purchased as is made an easy decoration.

Card 43 Christmas star ✶
Chipboard is excellent and I have left this star just as it comes. The background paper is a printed metallic 'wedding' paper.

Card 44 With love ✶
Chipboard again helping to cut my card in half.

Card 45 Silver heart ✶
The background paper here is very dominating. All I have added is a bit of ribbon tied around the layers and a heart which is actually a very large 'bead'.

Card 46 Love heart ✶
This heart is a beautiful die-cut picture. I have torn the edge on the handmade purple paper for a different effect. See page 28 tearing papers.

Paper tole

These are three dimensional pictures made from multi layers of paper. They make excellent card decorations.

See card 39 and page 50 for more on paper tole.

27

Ways to add interest to your layers

Accentuate the corners

Card 47 Good things come in small parcels ✿
Use very big corner stickers or multi layers of line stickers around the corners. See card 96 for multi lines.

Decorative scissors

Card 48 Dragon fly ✿
Trim your edges with decorative scissors or use fancy edge blades in a trimmer.

Compound layers
Compound layers can be most effective. Each layer is cut randomly and adhered to the one above. Work with bigger pieces than you need. Once it is joined as one piece, cut out to the required size.

Card 49 It's a girl thing ✿✿
Use a mixture of textures, colours and patterns for each layer. I have also added some edging to a couple of the layers.

Tear the edges
This is especially effective on papers with either a white or alternate core colour. Tear the paper toward you to reveal the core colour. Turn the paper as you go if you want all edges to show the white core.

Card 50 Thank you ✿✿
These strips have all had the edges torn to reveal the white core. I have also run a line of stitching around each strip. See page 80 for more on stitching.

Card 51 Tear away ✿✿
Each layer has been torn to reveal either the feathered edge or the core colour inside. I have added some fibre thread and lacy handmade paper. I had an off cut of the layered piece to add to the envelope.

TIP
For handmade or fibrous papers run a wet paintbrush along the line you want to tear. The paper will tear easily leaving a lovely feathered edge.

28

Decorate the edges of your layers
Use stickers, rub ons, braids, paper strips, lace, ric rac or ribbons. See card 49.

Distress the edges
Rub the edges with fine sandpaper to reveal the core colour. This gives an aged look to your papers. See card 36.

Ink the edges
Run an ink pad or a marker pen along the edge to leave rough shading. I keep only a few mini ink pads on hand. Gold, silver and sepia to age the edges of cardstock and papers. See page 39.

Decorate with pens
Ink writers: Use fine ink writing pens in various colours. Sepia is good for a heritage look. Run a wavy line along edges. Add some handwriting known as journaling.

Marker pens and gel pens: Doodle on papers with dots, wavy lines, swirls. Colour stickers with marker pens or gel pens.

Glitter glue: This is glitter in a glue base and is available in a large range of colours. You can draw swirls and write words leaving a glitter trail. Try to find one with a particularly fine nozzle as it will be much easier to manage.

Add highlights to all parts of your card with glitter glue including layers on your paper tole work. See more on page 51.

Card 52 Treasures of the heart ✿✿
The edge of my layer has a wriggly line of white gel pen. I have also added gel pen to each of the daisy shapes I have punched.

Card 51

Card 52

Decorating with Pens

29

What about punches?

Corner punches
A corner punch rounds or decorates the corner of your card or paper. Some only take a tiny nip out of the corner while others make a wide ark or fancy decorative patterns. One simple rounder is fine to start and not essential. It will give your corners a professional touch.

Card 53 Flower power ✽
All the layers have been rounded and even the card itself.

Card 54
Welcome to your new home ✽
A very ornate corner punch has been used here. This is actually a 'slot' corner punch. I have cut my plain background piece to fit the card front. Then I punched the corners with the slot punch. I cut the patterned centre piece big enough to slip into these corners like a photo. With so much interest in all the corners you only need something small in the centre. I have used a fold over punch to make the 3D daisy. I wrote the message on my computer in the circular form and punched it out with a circle punch.

Border punches
A border punch decorates the edge on your card or paper. Some punches are best on cardstock while others will only punch through paper. Scallops are very handy. You only need one to start.

Card 55 Glamarama ✽
I used my floral edge punch on one side of a dark pink paper. I used a scallop edge punch on a paler pink background. I then layered my print piece on the scalloped background and then onto the printed piece to get the double edging at the bottom.

NOTE: There are so many punches in the market place. If you like using punches find an ornate corner you enjoy using and a decorative one for the centre item. Flowers and butterflies will always be useful.

Nesting punches

These are very useful to have. Nesting means they are the same shape but vary in size so one fits inside the other. You can get a range of squares, circles, ovals and some with scalloped edges. You can mix and match as well.

A good starting size would be circles 1¼", 1½" and 1¾" and/ or squares 1", 1¼" and 1½".

They are handy for making little discs or medallions to offset a decorative piece on your card.

Card 56 Live love laugh

How easy is this. I used a beautiful piece of paper which needs very little else. I found wording on a circular sticker. I punched a cream scalloped circle and a gold plain circle to make a disc for the sticker.

Card 57 My hero

Edge your card with two strips of printed paper with a narrow paper edging strip. Punch three 1½" circles in plain card. Punch three 1¼" circles in patterned paper and make into discs. Decorate to suit.

Card 58 Cup cakes

The cup cakes are stickers. I made colour coordinating discs with my nesting punches. I added a colourful background including a die-cut felt strip. My message is a rub on. All have been foam mounted.

This card with its simple lines is very handy for a male card.

Card 59

Card 60

TIP: When punching flowers from patterned papers turn the punch over and line up with suitable prints.

Card 61

A set of flower punches

I would be lost without my flower punches and love to have a set of the same flower in varying sizes. Just look inside this book to see how often I use them.

My favourites are my regular, medium and large size DAISY and RETRO FLOWER.

Ideas with flower punches

Make paper poinsettias using two large and one medium daisy adhered with the petals alternating. Tease the petals to spread them and mount the triple flower on foam.

Use your flower punch to add interest to the edge of a layer on your card.

Card 59 Shop till you drop ✽

Simple use of flower punches, corner punches and nesting punches.

Card 60 I love you ✽

The two strips of paper, the message and the daisies were all cut from the one 12x12 sheet.

Card 61 Golden poinsettia ✽

A quick and easy card using a pre cut overlay and a beautiful piece of paper in the window. The poinsettia is elegant in gold or try red for the festive season.

Card 62 Fairyland ✽✽

Here I have punched a flower into the edge of my background. I have also made multi layers of my flower including one from acetate. See page 46 acetate. I have outlined all the punching with a white gel pen.

Card 62

TIP: If your large punches misbehave on light paper or fibrous papers, add a sheet of copy paper and punch through the double layer.

32

1/8" hole punch

This is invaluable for holes to thread ribbons through.

Card 63 With love ✽

Simple use of daisies on the centre line. I have punched a 1/8" hole in the tag message for the ribbon ties.

Paper Shaping Tool

With this simple little tool you can bring your papers to life by giving them dimension. You can improvise with a plastic teaspoon!

Paper shaping

Punch a flower shape and place it on a soft surface such as a computer mouse mat. Run the tool in a circular motion in the middle of the flower. The flower will begin to mould upwards.

Do the same on the petals and you will get a three dimensional flower developing.

I have then mounted them in threes and added a decoration to the centres. Actually the tops of split pins.

Card 64 Flower trio ✽✽

Punch three flowers in each of three sizes from coordinating papers. Follow the 3 steps shown.

TIP: Cut the back off split pins and mount them using a foam square.

33

There is no limit to what you can do with punches…

NOTE: Other handy punches include butterflies and leaves.

Card 65

TIP: If you are making a card just to have on hand, don't add the wording sticker until you need the card. Then you can use it for various occasions and customise it with the sticker.

Adding wording to your cards

Wording options are everywhere. Stickers, rub ons, actual items, stamps, old cards and magazines, ribbons to name a few. The wording can go straight onto your card or be layered separately and added with or without foam mounting. You can buy ready cut tags, use a tag punch or make your own tag shape for your wording.

Stickers

There are so many styles of stickers that will add a message to your cards. Some are actual items, some sheets of the same wording, others individual letters. They are available in all sizes, on cardstock, fabrics, typewriter discs and so on.

I have tried to include a good assortment throughout this book. See page 40 for more on stickers

Rub ons

These come on a clear film and are literally rubbed from the film sheet to your paper. You can get wording, pictures, swirls and patterns, edging, corners and more in single or multi colours. See card 34

Scrapbook sheets

These are an excellent source of wording.

Card 65 Congratulations ✻

All the decoration was taken from a scrapbook sheet.

Individual lettering

You can cut out your own letters from books and magazines or use alphabet stickers.

Card 66 Happiness ✻✻

Here I have made up my own message from individual sticker letters.

Dictionary meanings

Photocopy or scan a meaning direct from a dictionary and enlarge if necessary. Or make up your own and print from your computer.

Card 67 Cherish ✻

The picture has been taken from an old card and the wording scanned from the dictionary. I have added a little glitter glue to the tag and picture.

Card 67

Card 66

35

Do your own journaling

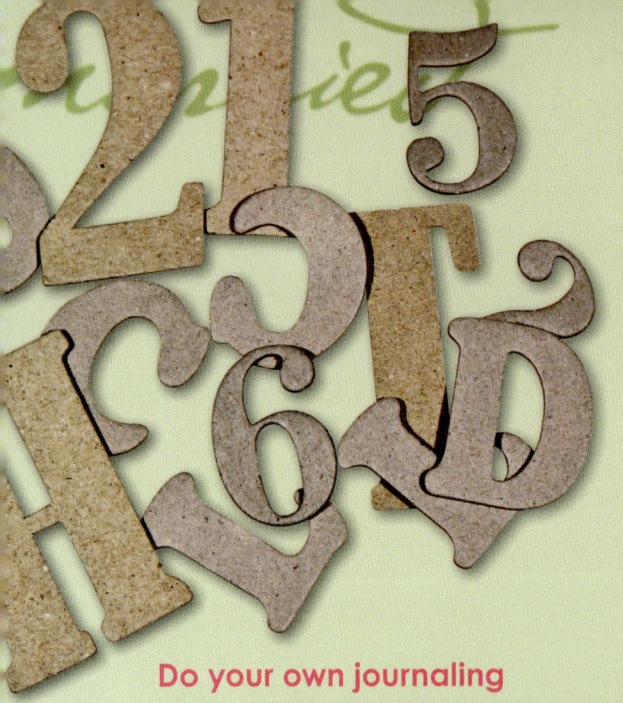

This is the term for using your own handwriting on your card. Many printed sheets have journaling on them.

If you are confident with your writing, it can look good and save you purchasing alternative wording. If you are not so confident, write on a separate piece of paper and add it to your card. If you make a mistake at least the whole card has not been ruined.

Card 68 **For you** ✽

I chose a printed paper with journaling in the design though it is not clear just what it says. I then wrote my message by hand on a separate piece of paper. Once I was happy with my writing, I layered it and added it to my card front. The heart is from a beading supplier.

Chipboard letters, numbers and decorative shapes

They can be used as they come (see cards 43 & 44). They can be painted, stamped or covered with paper. They are also useful as templates. You can add a single initial or write a whole word.

Card 69 **Baby** ✽✽✽

Cover the chipboard letters with your favourite paper, sand the edges, decorate and mount them on foam. I have also added a rub on.

Card 68

NOTE: Stamping is another whole world of wording and decorative opportunities and a craft in its own right. This book does not try to cover stamping. However, a few stamps with basic greetings and an ink pad can certainly get you started and assist with wording on your greeting cards.

TIP: I paint my letters with PVA glue mixed with a little water. Then I put the letter face down onto the back of my paper.

Make sure you are covering the correct side of your letter. Now leave till it is completely dry. Once dry, cut around each letter with a knife and then sand to get a tidy finish.

Card 69

pitter-patter of tiny feet...

37

Computer wording

Using your Computer

Print your own message on your computer. You can have your wording matching any colour. Print whole verses or individual words. See page 108 for my favourite fonts.

Card 70 Love kisses hugs ✽

The words were printed on my computer and mounted individually. I have edged the words with a white gel pen. There is also wording on the ribbon.

Card 71 Baby's christening ✽✽

Here I have printed the wording on overhead projector film. It is a clear sheet usually available at newsagents and office suppliers often by the sheet. You can layer this wording on top of other layers. I have edged the background layer with a scallop punch and added two fine border stickers.

Card 72 Santa Claus is coming ✽✽

Again I have used my computer to print my message, this time on trace paper. Trace paper is available from stationers and office supplies. 90gsm is best for printing. I have torn one edge and inked it with a silver ink pad. There is an adhesive available specifically for trace papers as most glues will show through. However, I use my narrow double sided tape sparingly and cover the edge with decoration. Here I have added some hand stitching in gold thread.

NOTE: The picture is from an old card. Copy it first for extra cards and add the glitter with your glitter glue.

TIP: I use PVA glue to hold this film in place. I put a tiny daub where the bow will go. PVA does dry clear but I still prefer to cover it with the bow.

Card 70

Card 72

Card 71

Invitations

Card 73 Paula and Michael
Here I have a small piece of beautiful Japanese print, a strip of gold metallic paper with a ribbon on top and a piece of cream metallic paper with the names printed in a beautiful font. All are mounted on a beige layer and then a base cream cardstock. Very simple but at the same time, very elegant.

Card 74 General invitation
The joy of using beautiful papers is that it is really all that you need. Here I have an A6 piece of plain cardstock. I have added a layer of beautiful specialty paper. I have printed my invitation from my computer onto metallic paper. Reserve any off cut strips to decorate the envelope. Quick. Easy. Effective.

Card 75 Jessie's 21st
The background is another beautiful sheet of handmade paper. It is not suitable to print on so I have used trace paper for the actual invitation. I have inked the edges with gold and trimmed the envelope with off cuts. The actual card is a base white cardstock DL size.

NOTE: Ink your paper by rubbing the stamp pad lightly along the edges.

39

More about stickers

The word 'sticker' encompasses a lot of product lines suitable for card making. You can get stickers in your grocery store, newsagents, dollar shops, wedding stationers and scrapbook stores. You can increase your colour range immensely by colouring in or over your stickers with pens, which are available at paper craft stores and newsagents.

Craft stickers

These are very popular stickers but sometimes they can distort when transferring long words from the sheet to the card. Using removable tape will help. It is sticky but will peel off without damaging your papers. Available at newsagents and general stationery stores.

Transferring craft stickers

Cut a piece of removable tape long enough to cover your wording.

Lift the tape while easing the sticker up onto it with your pricking tool.

It is now easy to decide where to place your wording. Position it on your card and peel off the tape.

Colouring craft stickers with permanent markers (colouring the actual sticker)

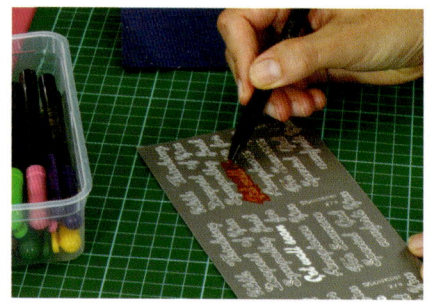

Using your marker pens, colour the whole word while still on the sheet.

Peel the words off the sheet with removable tape and add to your card.

Now you can have any colour sticker you like.

Colouring craft stickers with gel pens (colouring inside the sticker edges)

Adhere your sticker to card stock, vellum or acetate. Puddle the gel pen in a segment of your sticker. You are not actually colouring the sticker.

Gel pens work very well on acetate. Try blending the colours from one side of the space to the other. See page 46 for more on acetate.

Gel pens are wet ink and need time to dry. The colour develops and becomes more opaque as it dries.

Gel pens work well between the outlines of stickers; permanent markers produce solid colour over the surface

Border stickers

These are thin strips of stickers suitable to define edges and outline pictures. Very fine strips can be bent to outline curved shapes. Or, try using a fancy border sticker and cutting around the shape for an unusual edge.

Card 76 Be happy ✹✹

- Here I stuck an interesting border sticker to the front of the card and then cut around it for an uneven edge effect.
- I backed it with a different colour paper.
- I stuck a butterfly sticker on acetate and coloured it with my gel pens.
- When completely dry I cut around the shape and mounted it on foam squares.
- I also coloured other stickers flat on the card.
- I coloured the wording sticker with my permanent marker. See page 40.

Make your individual stickers 3D

Glue an individual sticker onto a firm background and cut it out. If appropriate, bend it for a 3D effect.

Card 77 Butterfly ✹

- This beautiful butterfly is a sticker. I put it onto acetate and then cut it out for a 3D effect. You could also put it on light cardstock and cut around the shape for a similar effect.
- I have mounted it on a medley of circular items. A gold circular sticker on a punched circle of gold paper. This is on a punched scalloped circle in purple. The outline in black is a rub on.
- The decorative lacy strips on the card are actually just paper strips from a 12x12 sheet.

It may sound tricky but this is in fact a very easy card.

Card 78 Christmas bauble ✹

The bauble is actually two glitter stickers back to back. I have cut out the bauble shape, tied twine to it and left it hanging free on the card. Now it can be easily removed as a tree decoration. Just punch a 1/8th hole in the card front and tape the twine inside the card with removable tape.

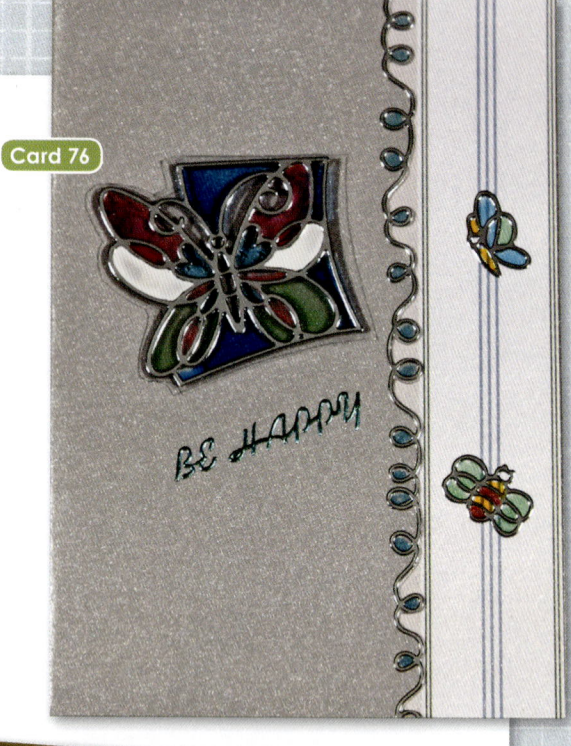

Clear stickers

Many sticker sheets are 'clear' stickers. The colour of the paper you stick it to will show through a clear film.

Card 79 Little pink dress ✿✿

The dress and accessories were all clear stickers put onto the same pink silk paper and then cut out. I used two strips of the same pink silk either side of the card front and a couple of border stickers.

Framing stickers

These are also clear. You can pop a picture onto your paper and then stick the frame over it like a window.

Card 80 Christmas trio ✿

I selected three small die-cut pictures. I sat them on the gold metallic paper and put a framing sticker over each of them. The frames have a clear window in the centre. I then cut out each shape and foam mounted them on my centre line.

3D sticker sheets

Some stickers sheets are meant for 3D work. The shapes are similar but in different sizing.

Card 81 Heartbeat ✿✿

This card used one entire 3D sticker sheet. All the components were on the one sheet. I stuck the four shapes onto alternate coloured metallic papers, cut each out and then mounted them on top of each other with foam mount. I completed the card with the corner stickers and extra shapes from the sheet.

Card 82 Oh Christmas tree ✿✿

This too is a sticker sheet with similar sticker shapes in varying sizes. Ideal for 3D mounting. I stuck three different size trees to hologram paper. I cut each out, folded them in half and mounted them on each other along the fold line, with narrow double sided tape. The stars and dots also came from this sheet. The extra little tag is attached with a split pin.

NOTE: Hologram paper is available at craft stores where craft sticker sheets are sold.

Negative stickers as a background

This is making use of the bits left on your sticker sheet after using the main sticker shape. They can be very useful for filling a background.

Card 83 Angel ★★

The border sticker I used on my angel Christmas card left behind all these little dots. I have used the grid on my mat to help align them on the background. Quite effective! The lovely olde angel was from a poster.

Card 84 White daisies by Ellen ★

The daisy centres and background decoration are taken from leftover pieces on sticker sheets.

Card 83

Card 84

Negative stickers for 3D

You can also make your butterfly sticker three dimensional by picking up the negative bits.

Transferring the butterfly (For full steps see card 85)

Pick up all the negative pieces of your butterfly using removable tape.

Transfer them to a piece of paper and add any bits you may have left behind.

Now position the main butterfly over the negative one and trace the outline. Cut the negative one out and adhere under the main butterfly along the body section.

Card 85 Butterfly ✹✹✹

- Stick your butterfly onto the paper of your choice and cut it out.
- Now cover all the negative pieces left behind with removable tape. You may have to overlap strips of tape if the butterfly is a big one.
- Using your pricking tool tease each piece of sticker onto the tape. It is a bit tedious and I sometimes miss a few bits, but do not worry. You can add them in later once you have most lifted.
- Now stick these pieces onto a second sheet of paper in a complementing colour and add any bits you left behind.
- Position the original butterfly over the bits and trace the outline shape around the bits.
- Cut out the second butterfly and mount the first on top of the second just along the body for your 3D effect.

The layering of this card is shown in card 16.

NOTE: You can buy removable transfer sheets at craft stores and cut them to the size of your sticker shape.

Card 85

45

Chapter 4 ❋ What about these?

What is acetate?

Acetate is clear plastic sheeting. You will often get pieces in packaging and they are handy to keep. If you want to buy acetate, I prefer to buy overhead projector film 100 microns. It can be purchased at office supply stores and newsagents often by the individual sheet. It can then be printed on. Make sure you purchase to suit your printer, either inkjet or laser.

Ideas for using acetate

- You can give your stickers a 3D effect by mounting them on acetate.
- You can colour the stickers with gel pens on acetate.
- Clear stickers on acetate let the background show through.
- Put your sticker onto the acetate and then cut it out. It is not necessary to be too exact as the acetate edges do not show.
- You can print your own pictures, photos or wording onto the film and use them on your cards.
- You can often buy 12x12 sheets of acetate already printed.

Card 87

Card 86

Card 88

Card 86 Church window ✱
This is a clear sticker on acetate. I cut it out and mounted it on foam. The lovely white silk paper layer shows through.

Card 87 Missing you ✱
Here I have used two clear stickers on acetate. I cut each out and mounted one on top of the other with foam. It can be tricky to hide the foam mount. I put rhinestones in the corners to hide the foam squares underneath. Alternatively I could have coloured the stickers with my gel pens.

Card 88 Flower wheel ✱
These too are stickers on acetate. I have again mounted one on top of the other with foam.

Card 89 Dragonfly ✱
This is from a pre-printed 12x12 acetate sheet. My background layer is showing through the acetate.

Card 90 Rose lady ✱
This is a picture I have printed onto acetate and put onto my card with split pins.

Acetate as your cardstock

Card 91 Bird in a cage ✱
You can use the acetate as your actual card. I have cut a piece A5 and folded it in half. I have decorated the front with ribbons and flowers and added a single piece of cardstock to the centre as the insert.

Punching acetate
Punch shapes out of acetate and then decorate with gel pens, markers or stickers. See card 62.

47

What is vellum?

The word vellum is often misleading. True vellum is animal hide. Manuscripts were written on vellum in days prior to paper supplies. However, we use the term today for a semi opaque sheet of paper. This sheeting is also referred to as parchment or trace paper. Vellum comes in many thicknesses and has a white core when torn, pricked with a needle or stretched. It is used for the gorgeous craft of Pergamano where patterns are pricked with needles and the vellum is stretched with various tools to reveal the white core. Google 'pergamano'.

From a card maker's perspective it is a wonderful medium for decorating cards as it is available plain or in many prints. It can be printed on with a home computer, though some brands will let the ink bleed so always test first. It is used a lot in the wedding invitation industry for a semi-sheer overlay.

Card 92 Michelle and Shaun

This style of invitation is very economical to produce. The background card is DL size. An A4 sheet will cut into three this size. The coloured sheet with the invitation printed on it is a metallic paper. The top sheet is a printed trace paper. The three layers are held together with a brad or split pin.

Card 93 Purple daisies

This is a white card 130mm square. I have wrapped a lilac silk paper right across the back and 30mm onto the front. I have tucked the daisy printed trace paper under the silk. The trim is a short piece of ribbon in a small buckle.

Card 94 World peace

This is a picture from an old card layered onto a 130mm square card. Before attaching it, I have torn a piece of printed trace paper to cover half the picture. I have used narrow double sided tape to hold it in place and run a line of stitching right around. A few beads trim the corner.

Card 95 Lots of love

I have stuck this sticker to vellum and coloured the flower with my gel pens. I have puddled the gel and blended the colours in each section of the sticker. I then cut out the individual flower and mounted it on my card front.

NOTE: There is a vellum glue available from paper craft stores that will not show through vellum if you prefer.

TIP: When printing on vellum from an inkjet printer the ink can sometimes 'bleed' into the paper, so always test first. Laser printers do not cause this issue.

Card 93

Card 94

49

TIP: Use your pricking tool to lift foam squares onto your papers and to remove the backing pieces.

What is paper tole?

This is a craft in itself and I am only going to touch briefly on it in relation to our card making. Paper tole is making three dimensional pictures by building up layers of the same picture. True craftsmen would use a moulding tool to shape the papers, a thick glue to help mound the shapes and many, many layers, often finishing with a varnish.

For card making there are usually only three to four layers separated by foam mount. At craft stores you can buy sheets or even booklets full of pictures suitable for paper tole. Some have the layers decided for you and even numbered while others go so far as to die-cut the pictures so you only have to push out the pieces and mount them. **For quick and easy cards, these die-cut ones are wonderful.**

NOTE: Foam mount can be bought in varying thicknesses. I use 1, 2 and 3mm foam. The more paper layers you have, the thinner the foam needs to be or your picture will end up too bulky to post. It is available in sheets, rolls, cut into strips, circles, squares and even tiny 2mm dots. If starting out I would get 2mm thick in 5mm squares.

Card 96

Card 96 Iris ★★

This is made up from a die-cut sheet of pictures with the numbers to guide you.

- Push out each piece starting with no. 1, the biggest.
- Adhere this first layer to your background layer.
- Push out piece no. 2 and add foam squares to the back of it. See steps below.
- Peel off the backings of the foam squares and with your tweezers, hold piece no. 2 until it is exactly over the same section of piece no 1 and adhere it on top.
- Repeat with pieces 3 and 4.
- Now mount your completed picture onto your card front.

NOTE: Position your foam squares approximately 15mm apart making sure not to be too close to the paper edge or it may be seen. Also make sure any narrow strips of your picture have a foam support under them. You may need to cut some of the foam pieces to get it small enough to fit. You need the whole picture supported all over if possible.

TIP: If you are cutting the picture yourself, note just how small the pieces will actually be. Some can get very fiddly.

Building your paper tole pictures

Remove the first two pictures from the paper tole die-cut sheet or cut out yourself if not die-cut.

Adhere the first picture to your background layer and add mounting squares to the back of the second picture.

Position it exactly on top of your first layer. Repeat for the remaining layers to build up your complete picture.

50

Card 97 Ballerina ✿✿

This was from a die-cut sheet and done in the same way as the iris. Picture I included the background unlike the iris.

I have added glitter glue to the ballerina's skirt for a touch of sparkle. The lacy edge is a sticker.

Card 98 Ballerina Kyela ✿✿

Paper tole pictures can be actual items. Here I have printed the face of my granddaughter and put it on the last layer of the paper tole. Instead of adhering the ballerina to the card, I have attached a piece of ribbon between the layers so it can easily be removed from the card and played with or kept as a memento. Just punch a 1/8" hole in the card front and tape the ribbon inside the card with removable tape.

TIP: Paper tole pictures are great for card making. It is good to make up a few pictures and have them ready to just pop on a card when you need one in a hurry.

DECORATING IDEA: Add glitter glue to your finished piece.

Children love it when you can incorporate their photo into a card

51

Make your own paper tole pictures

If you have your own printer you can make your own colour paper tole pictures by copying the same picture three or four times and deciding on the layers yourself. Imagine what part of the picture is in the background and which parts would be closer to you if the scene were real.

Use good quality copy paper and select 'best' copy quality on your printer options.

Card 99 My friend ★★★

This was an old card I particularly liked. I reduced it to fit my folded A5 cardstock and copied it four times:

- Layer 1 is the full picture on a plain background layer.
- Layer 2 is the two girls in full.
- Layer 3 is the girls dresses and heads.
- Layer 4 is their hair and hat.

You make your own choices on the number of layers and just what to include.

Card 100 Maureen's snowdrop ★★★

My friend Maureen purchased this beautiful figurine as a gift. She copied a picture of it and made a matching card in paper tole. What a lovely idea!

Card 101 Rose buds ★★★★

You can buy printed cards and then use them over and over for your own paper tole cards. Reduce them and copy the pictures three or four times. Complete in the same way as card 99. For the rose buds I have used three layers and mounted the whole lot onto a background layer.

Card 102 Cup cake ★★★★

Done the same as 101 with some glitter glue and rhinestones for the bling.

52

Pyramid pictures

Paper tole has many variations and pyramid pictures is one. Pyramids are three dimensional pictures and are very handy on cards as they are quick to put together. Again you can buy sheets of these at craft stores or print your own.

Instead of cutting out the actual shapes in the picture, each layer simply trims the whole picture smaller in standard shapes like squares, rectangles, stars, hexagons.

Imagine your original picture is 50mm square:

- Layer 1 is the full 50x50mm square
- Layer 2 is say 45x45mm square. Just take 2.5mm off all sides of the original picture.
- Layer 3 is 40x40mm and so on to actually form a pyramid.

Card 103 Cleopatra ✹✹

This is from a bought sheet. There are six layers to this picture so I used my 1mm foam squares to keep it from being too high. Each layer is the star shape coming in smaller and smaller.

Card 104 TLC ✹✹

A variation on pyramids is twisted pyramids. Each picture is a rectangle getting smaller and smaller but the image has been twisted for an interesting effect. This is using a bought sheet. I doubt I could make my own and get the twist!

Card 103

Card 104

Pyramid pictures are a variation on paper tole

53

Paper napkins

Paper napkins are a wonderful source of beautiful paper designs. You can use the actual napkin or copy the designs onto good quality paper.

Using the actual napkin

Card 105 Happy retirement ✶✶

The napkin is usually 2 or 3 actual layers and you only want the top printed layer. So first peel off the plain layers.

- Now cut out the section of the picture you plan to use allowing extra all round.
- Select cardstock to back the napkin and also cut it bigger than you need. We will trim it later.
- Mix PVA glue with a tiny bit of water, just enough so you can cover the entire card quickly using a paintbrush.
- Carefully spread the napkin onto the cardstock and using a dry cloth smooth out any wrinkles. If you have a brayer (roller tool) now is the time to use it.
- Allow it to dry completely and keep it flat. I sit a piece of glassine paper on top and then a heavy book.
- Once dry, mark your cutting lines for the actual size you plan to use. I use a pencil and cut with scissors as a knife will often tear the napkin layer.
- Mount on an extra layer and then onto your card and decorate.

Card 106 le Papillon ✶✶

This card is made in the same way as card 105 but I inked the edges. The napkin soaks up the ink in interesting ways. I also cut out a butterfly shape from the napkin and adhered it only along the body for a 3D effect.

Card 107 Congratulations ✶✶

Same technique. I just love the beautiful designs.

NOTE: Gluing onto textured cardstock gives the napkin layer an interesting effect.

NOTE: Glassine is a paper similar to greaseproof kitchen paper. PVA glue will not stick to it so it makes a good shield if PVA is drying under a weight to keep it flat. Art suppliers should carry it.

Card 105

Card 106

Card 107

Brayer

54

Using napkin pictures

Card 108 Peace and joy ✿✿

The Santa on this card was found on a napkin along with other suitable pictures. I copied the picture and mounted it on several layers with stitching.

Using napkin patterns

Napkin patterns are also useful as pictures to copy. Scan in and experiment with reducing the size to suit your card, then print them out.

Card 109 Red silhouette ✿

I reduced this napkin and copied it to good quality paper. It makes a lovely background.

Card 110 Penny for your thoughts ✿

This black and white pattern I reduced to 70%, 50% and 30% and printed out. I cut out the actual pattern and mounted each layer on top of the other with foam mount. I thank Penny for this idea.

Card 111 Daisy blue ✿✿

The blue flowers I have reduced to 70% and copied 3 times. This has been worked as paper tole cutting away a little more picture on each layer.

55

Chapter 5 ✱ Folding your cards

Simple folds

What about different ways to fold your cards? So far most of the cards have been a single and complete fold either landscape, portrait or square. Let's consider a few variations on this.

Paper wrap

Why not fold the decorative paper and then put the card inside?

Card 112 I believe ✱

Fold a beautiful piece of paper in half and put your cardstock on the inside. Hold it in place with a strip of double sided tape high on the back and the ribbon tie on the front. Leave the paper short by 20mm for the cardstock colour to show.

Colour the sticker with a permanent marker pen.

Shorten one side

Cutting one side of your card short can allow something on the insert to show through to the front.

Card 113 Rebecca & Lachlan ✱

The names on the front are part of the actual invitation inside.

Centre opening cards

Card 114 Love you ✱

This style card is handy to use up long strips of cardstock. The cardstock is a 300x100mm strip. The opening can be right in the middle or offset as in this card. The message disc helps to hold it closed.

Card 115 Good luck ✱

DL or square centre openings are good for invitations. You only need a single insert sheet inside. You will however need something to hold the card shut. A ribbon tie, a buckle or an object to overlap the two edges. Even a slot to tuck a flap into. In this sample I have opted for a buckle and ribbon.

Card 116 True friendship ✱

This selection of papers and tags were all from the same 12x12 sheet. The lace trim is a sticker. I have used the central tag to overlap the opening.

Overlap the fold

This makes it so much easier to keep a centre opening card closed. Have your fronts overlap by 30 to 40mm.

Card 117 Gold daisy ✱

My card stock is 290x130mm. (not quite half a 12x12) The two ends are each folded in 80mm to overlap each other.

This is also an economical use of the specialty paper as I have only added it to the top section.

Card 115

Card 114

NOTE: This lovely paper layer in card 114 is termed "artist papers". These are prints from artists' work. Look for them online.

Love You!

Card 116

True friendship

needs no words...

Card 117

Happy Birthday

57

'A' frame or notebook style

These also use up long strips of cardstock. Fold your card in half but make it notebook style.

Card 118 Cuddles ✤✤

- I have used an off cut 210x80mm.
- I have folded it in half and made a spine by taping the top 20mm together.
- I punched two 1/8" holes and tied with ribbon.
- I only used a single sheet for my insert and scalloped the lower edge with a border punch. I attached the insert before I taped the spine together.
- For decoration see card 151. Note the envelope trim.

Card 119 Anniversary ✤

This is again using an offcut 300x100mm folded in half. I again made a spine but it can be left 'A' frame. Decorate as you wish.

Fold back the front

Card 120 Fans ✤

- Fold your card in half and then fold the front back on itself.
- Attach decorative items to the fold line so they sit centrally on your card. I have used clear fan stickers on two different coloured cardstock and cut them out.
- I added a thin strip of beautiful paper top and bottom of the card and some corner and border stickers.

Trifold card

Card 121 Celebrate ✤✤

- This card is 300x150mm. (Half a 12x12)
- I have folded it 100mm from each end concertina style.
- I decorating the front panel and then cut around the image of the tree. I then added some multi layer daisies.

Little is nice

Make tiny cards for little people or as gift tags.

Card 122 Little is nice ✤

- My card is only 80x55mm.
- I added a decorative insert.
- I punched decorative corners to reveal the insert.
- Make your own envelope and decorate to match. For template see page 109. Resize as required.

Card 121

Simple wallet

Card 123 Daisy wallet ✿✿

This card can be made any size. You need your cardstock longer than twice the width. It is good to use up strips of cardstock. See diagram for card 123.

- My cardstock is 205x90mm.
- Fold the cardstock at a point equal to the width of the card. I have folded at 90mm to form a square.
- Now trim any overhang to form a flap and fold it over. I have a 25mm flap and have shaped the corners.
- Mark with a pencil 2 positions for holes on the flap and punch with your 1/8" punch.
- Mark on the front where these holes align and punch again. You can trim the holes with eyelets or circular stickers and tie with twine or ribbon.
- Add your decoration.

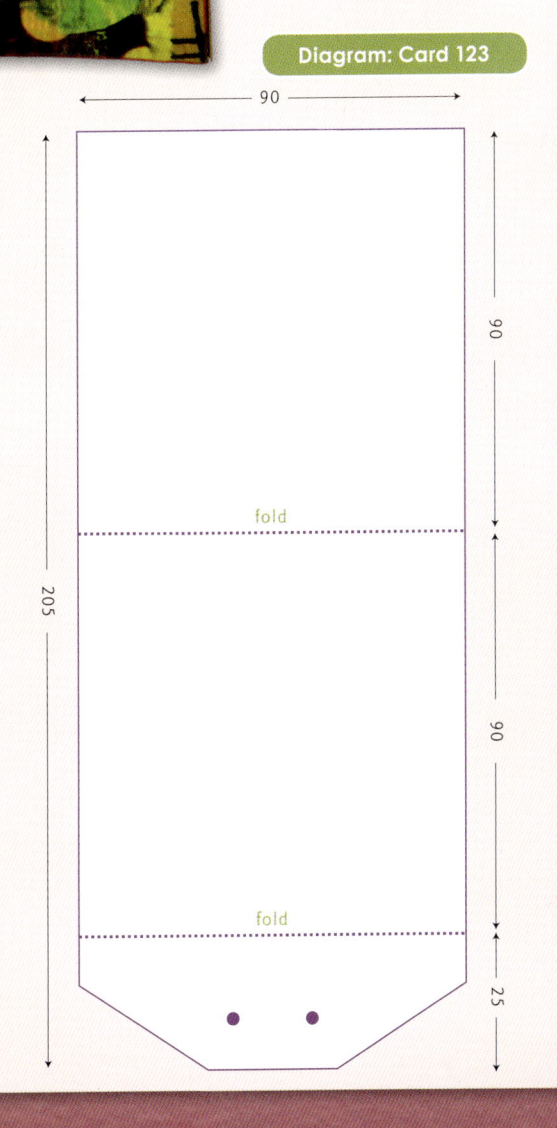

Diagram: Card 123

Card 123

59

Unusual folds

Lets get a bit more fancy with our folds! Some of these may not be so quick and easy but very nice!

Vertical folds

Card 124 My Picasso ✹✹

- Cut cardstock to A5. You will also need another square piece 65x65mm for the front. It does not have to be the same colour.
- With the front of your cardstock facing you, score 45mm from each end and valley fold.
- Now score 30mm in from the first folds and mountain fold.
- Decorate the side panels but be mindful of just what will show when the card is folded.
- Decorate the separate front square and adhere to the front panel on the diagonal.

NOTE: You could fold in the same manner and add a round disc to the front instead.

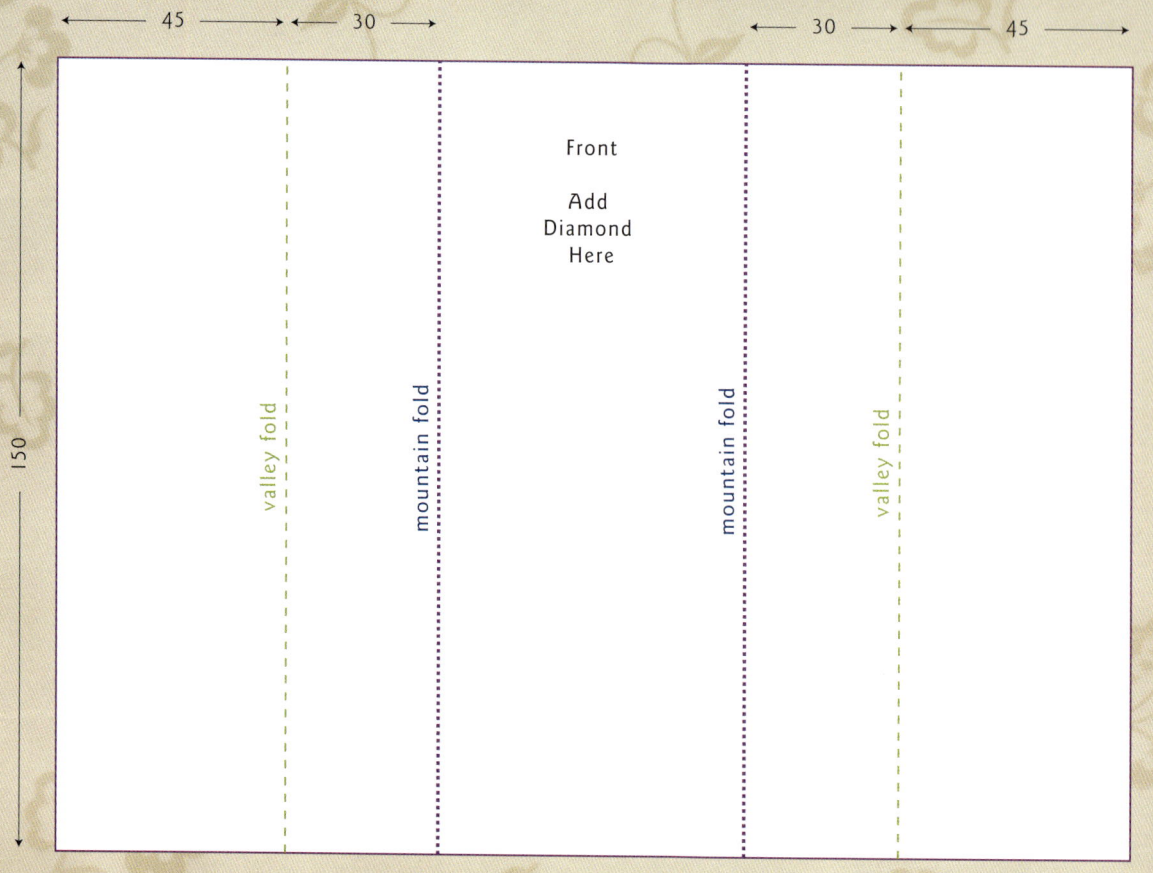

Card 124

← 45 → ← 30 →   ← 30 → ← 45 →

Front

Add Diamond Here

valley fold | mountain fold | mountain fold | valley fold

150

← 210 →

60

Diamond folds

Card 125 Party time ✦✦✦✦

This card relies on accurate fold lines to look good.

- Start with cardstock 210x140mm. This will fit a C6 envelope.
- Working on the back of your cardstock, score the centre line lengthwise and fold in.
- Score 70mm from the top and fold down.
- Mark a point X on the centre fold 20mm below this horizontal fold line.
- Mark two points Y on each side 50mm below the horizontal fold line.
- Score the two lines X to Y and fold back. This is somewhat tricky. Just get them lightly folded in the backward direction.
- Hold your card with these folds heading back from point X and the top coming forward and close your card. It will pull into a diamond on top.
- Crease all fold lines to make sharp.
- Decorate as you wish.
- An insert shaped to fit is nice inside.

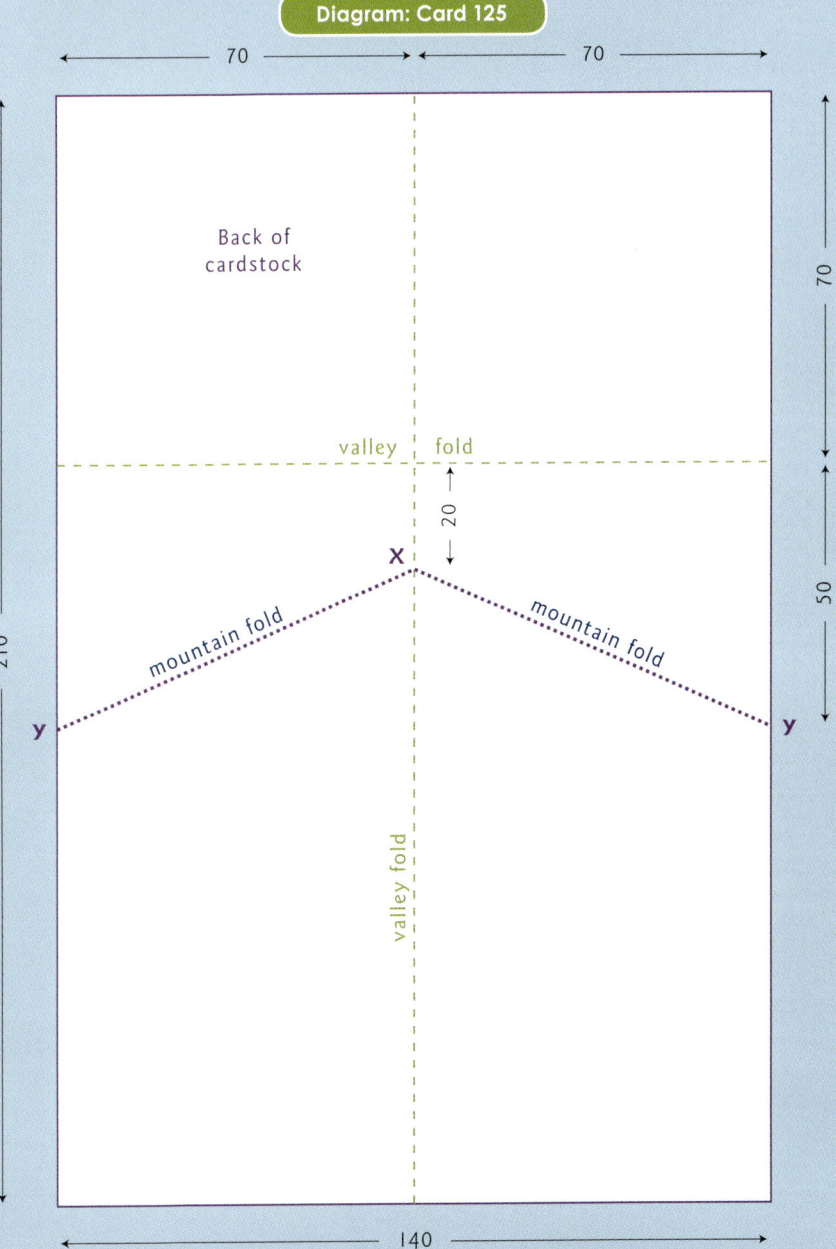

Card 125

Insert

Diagram: Card 125

70 — 70

Back of cardstock

valley fold

20

X

mountain fold — mountain fold

y — y

valley fold

210

70

50

140

Card 126
Double diamond birthday ✦✦✦✦

This is a double version of card 125.

- Start with cardstock 250x130mm. The finished card will fit into a C6 envelope.
- Working on the back of your cardstock, score the centre line and fold in.
- Score 65mm from both ends and fold in.
- Mark two points X and four points Y as per diagram 126.
- Score the four lines X to Y and fold back.
- Still working from the back, with these fold lines going back and the top and bottom folds coming forward, fold the card in along the centre fold.
- It will pull into the double diamond.
- Decorate as you wish.

Diagram: Card 126

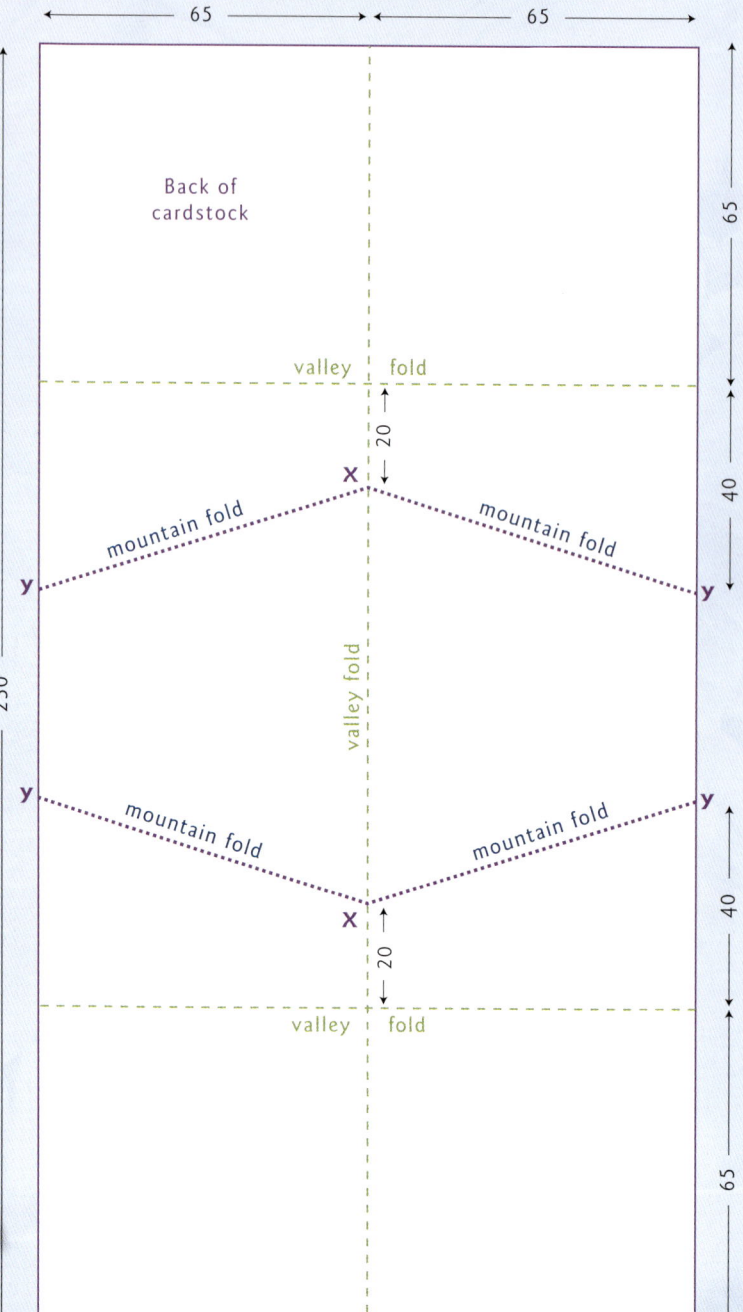

Back of cardstock

65 | 65 | 65 | 40 | 20 | 250 | valley fold | mountain fold | X | Y

Card 127

Concertina folds

Concertina cards are really just oversize cards or multi page cards. Try to have a theme to your pages and a flow of design. Something that is repeated throughout the pages to make each page relate to the rest.

Card 127 Best wishes ✿✿

- My cardstock is 300x120mm.
- Fold the card in half then fold each half back on itself.
- Round the corners with your corner rounder punch. I punched through double folds of cardstock with the pages together.
- The ribbon ties were attached under the decorative paper square on the front.
- The internal decoration is all from a sticker sheet with a few pearls for trim.

Card 128 In vogue ✿✿✿✿

Adding more pages can turn your card into a book. I have used cardstock for the entire book.

- My book is 420x110mm. If you need to join two pieces together, try to do so on a fold and overlap 10mm.
- I have folded each page 70mm wide.
- I have layered the front page with a ribbon caught under the layers to hold the whole book together.
- Decorate each page and even the back cover.

Card 128

63

Card 129 The Ooslem bird ✤✤✤✤

This is a very old poem my grandfather used to recite. If you have any such special memory you would like to include in a card or book form, a concertina card works very well.

- For this card, as there would be many pages and I wanted to print them on my computer, I used A4 paperweight inside and cardstock for the covers.

- My pages are 105mm high and folded to make them 74mm wide. I joined pages with a 10mm overlap on a fold.

- The number of pages will vary depending on what you want to write.

- Concertina the pages to a finished size of 105x74mm with a blank page front and back.

- Cut two pieces of cardstock for the covers 110x80mm.

- Cover the front with a decorative layer concealing a ribbon tie.

- Decorate an envelope to match.

NOTE: You could cover two pieces of cardboard with decorative paper like covering a school book then insert the concertina pages inside these two covers.

Handy hints:

- Set out your printing such that you can concertina into a series of pages.

- Remember to allow a 10mm overlap on the fold to join pages.

- A mock book is handy until you are sure just what will be on each page. This printing setup diagram for an A4 page may guide you.

- If this is all too tricky for you, make your book up with blank pages. Then print each page individually and adhere the writing to each page.

Card 129

	74	74	74	74
105	Inside front cover	Middle text pages		Inside back cover
Cut in half				
105	Leave Blank	Middle text pages		Leave Blank

64

Card 130 Graduation ★★★★

This is a concertina card enclosed in a box rather than flat covers. I allowed two extra blank pages front and back so my decoration would not start until the folds were out of the box.

- I used paper for the concertina as I had a lot of pages.
- Each page is 40x40mm.
- Each page was decorated with a letter sticker on 2 layers.
- I made a box 50mm square following Box 14 on page 102.
- I added a top to the box 70mm square decorated with red thread tied to a gold jump ring. (from bead suppliers)
- The front and back pages of the concertina were adhered inside the bottom of the box and inside the lid.

Card 130

65

Sequence fold 1

These are good for invitations as you can add a square card inside with the invitation details. They are quite quick and easy to make.

Card 131 Silver night

- Cut paper or light card 200x200mm. I have used printed metallic paper 120gsm.
- Now cut a 50x50mm square out of each corner.
- Fold the four flaps formed into the centre one after the other and lock the last one under the first. I use the grid on my mat to keep it all square. Use your bone folder to crease sharp fold lines.

I defined each edge with a thin strip of black paper and a string of daisies.

See diagram for card 131.

Card 132 Silver bouquet

This is the same as Card 131 but I rounded one corner of each flap with my corner punch and defined the edges with bendable border stickers. The bouquet is a sticker.

Card 133 Daisy blossom

This is the same as card 131 but slightly smaller. 180x180mm with the cut out corners only 45x45mm.

My paper was from a 12x12 print. I attached my daisy trio decoration to one flap only on mounting foam.

NOTE: The corners you cut out are 1/4 the length of the initial square. So start with a size square that easily divides by four.

Card 134 Red roses

This card is done in exactly the same way as the above but I have rounded each flap with my circle cutter.

NOTE: When tying bows, put the left piece over the right piece to start, then tie the right loop over the left loop. This way your bow will always sit well on your card.

Sequence fold 2

Card 135 Wedding rings ✦✦✦✦

This card is a little more involved but well worth the effort. It is a fun card for your friends to receive as it is a little puzzling to open. You can make it any size you like but remember your envelope size.

- Cut your cardstock 100x100mm. This is the size of your finished card.
- On the back put pencil lines to divide the back into four squares 50x50mm. It is important when adding the paper flaps to keep them very square on the back so they fold neatly onto the front. Your pencil lines will help.
- You now need 4 strips of paper 210mm long and 50mm wide. Select four different colours that coordinate. I have used plain and printed metallic papers 120gsm.
- Glue the strips to the back of the card as in diagram 135. Each one is glued to one square only:
  - Glue strip 1 to square 1 overlapping square 4
  - Glue strip 2 to square 2 overlapping square 1
  - Glue strip 3 to square 3 overlapping square 2
  - Glue strip 4 to square 4 overlapping square 3.
- Turn the card over and fold each flap down in sequence and tuck the last one into the first. Trim off any excess on each flap.
- Add a text sheet to the inside of your card.

Card 136 Double hearts ✦✦✦✦

Completed in the same way as card 135 but I have used double sided 12x12 coordinating papers.

These give an interesting effect when opened showing the reverse patterns.

NOTE: For a neat finish it is best to have each flap just a bit longer than required and trim back once the card is folded. I have allowed an extra 10mm in the measurement above.

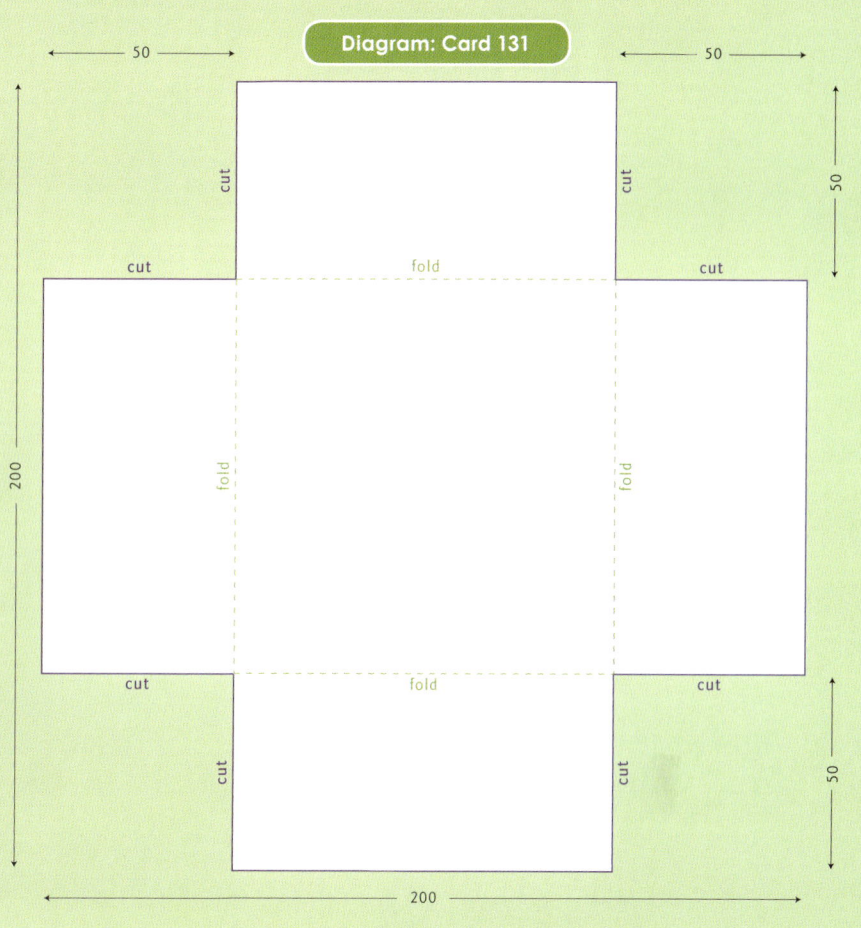

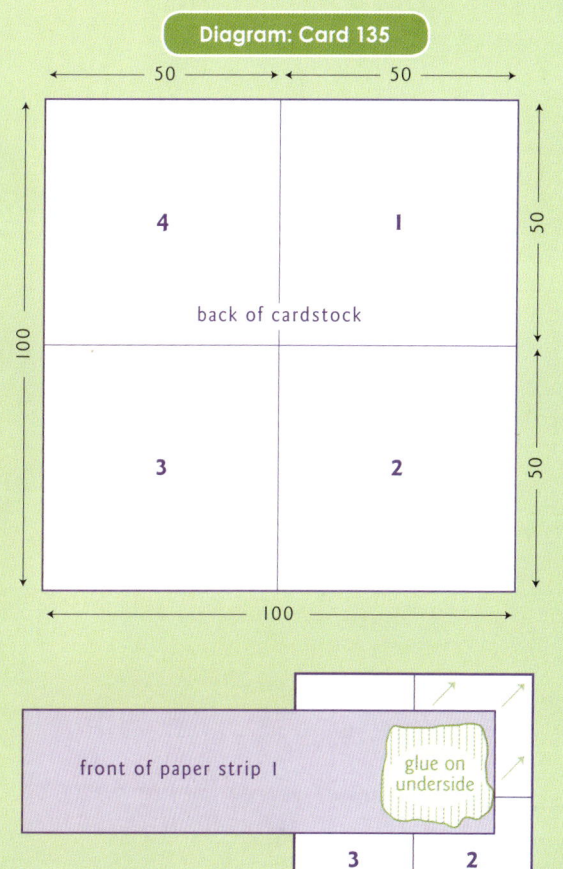

67

Chapter 6 ✽ How to add more interest

Basic card shapes

What about shapes? There is no limit to the shapes you can make your card but again start with your envelope and work the shape from there.

Triangle

This is the ideal shape for a Christmas tree of course.

Card 137 Oh Christmas tree ✽

Fold an A5 in half. Measure the spine. Measure the same distance from the top of the spine down the open side and put a pencil mark at X. Cut from the top and bottom of the spine to this point. See diagram 137.

My tree is decorated using a sticker sheet designed for 3D work. See page 43 on stickers.

Circle

This can be an almost full circle or just a rounding of one side into an arc. See diagram 138.

Card 138 Good luck ✽✽

Fold your cardstock to form a square card. Use a circle cutter to trim the edge off your card. You can just curve the edge or make it almost a round card depending on the arc taken. Remember to leave a reasonable spine for the card to fold on. Mine is 60mm long and I started with a square 130x130mm.

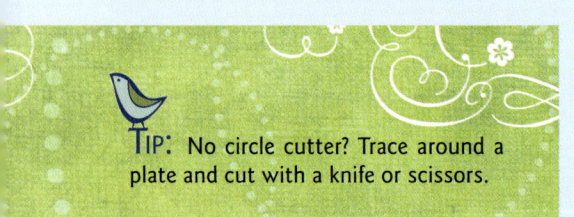

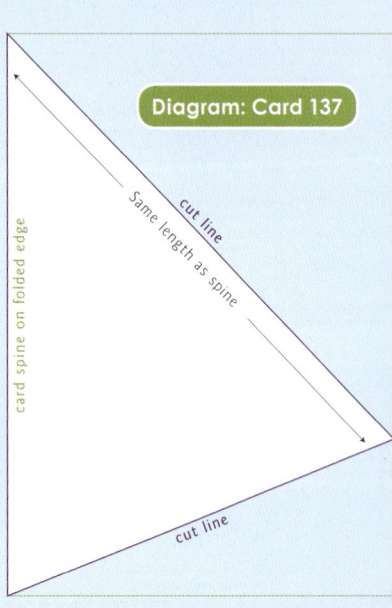

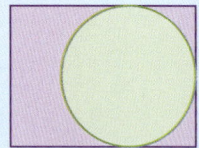

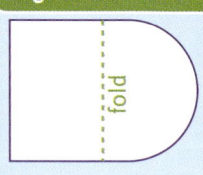

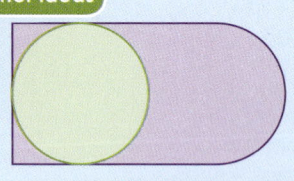

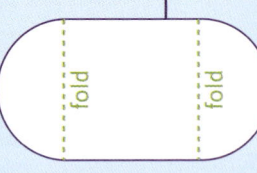

TIP: No circle cutter? Trace around a plate and cut with a knife or scissors.

Card 137

Diagram: Card 137
cut line
Same length as spine
card spine on folded edge
cut line

Card 138

Diagram: Card 138 & Other ideas

Round the end on a rectangular card.　　Fold a centre opening card and round the fronts.

Tags

A tag is simply a rectangular piece of card with one end shaped. The end can be cut quite pointed or a gentle rounding. They often include a hole and a tie. They can be any size. They make a nice card idea if included in their own holder or sleeve.

Card 139 Happy birthday ★★

- My tag is 110x60mm with all four corners rounded and the edges inked.
- I inked the edge of a 50x20mm piece of card, punched three 1/8" holes across the centre and tied ribbons. I then adhered this to the top of the tag.
- For the sleeve I cut a piece of cardstock 200x80mm.
- I scored a fold line 110mm from one end and folded.
- I used a decorative corner punch on the two higher corners.
- I inked all the edges and then adhered the sides together and decorated with punched shapes, stickers and rhinestones.

Card 140 You're invited ★★★★

- I have cut five tags 180, 160, 140, 120 and 100mm long and all 75mm wide in cardstock of various colours.
- Each had a 10mm snip off the top corners, 1/8" holes with sticker surrounds and gold twine.
- Each tag could have a printed layer for the invitation, accommodation, gift register, RSVP details and so on.
- I made a sleeve to hold the tags from clear vellum (90gsm). See diagram 140.
- I printed the names on the vellum then aligned the template over the wording before cutting out.
- I glued the vellum with double sided tape on the back where it could not be seen.
- I decorated with double heart rhinestone stickers available at wedding stationers.

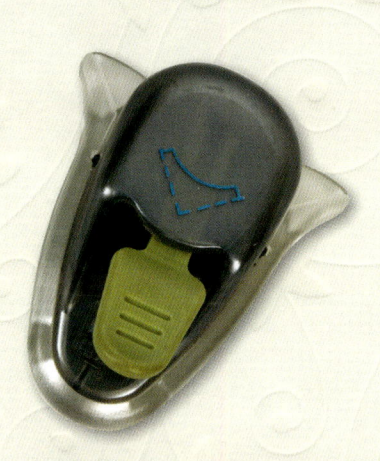

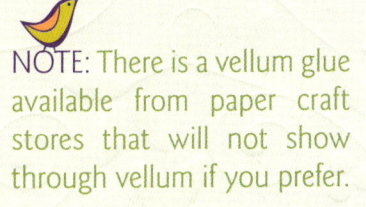

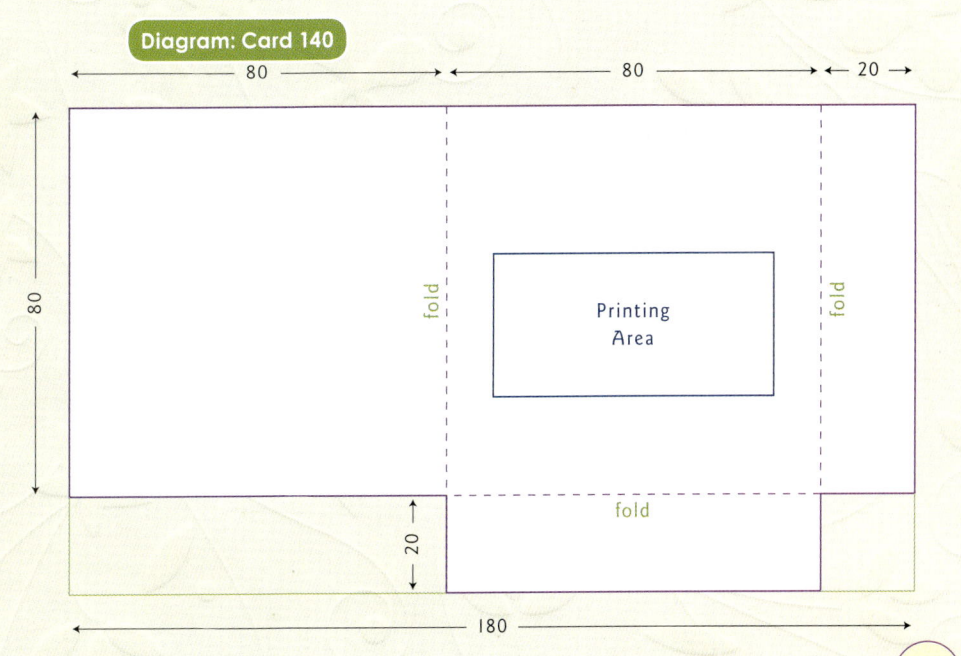

NOTE: There is a vellum glue available from paper craft stores that will not show through vellum if you prefer.

Diagram: Card 140

Templates for shapes

Card 141 Handbag ✸✸

See template on page 110. Resize to suit. Trace pattern onto cardstock. Fold and decorate.

To keep the top flap closed I have rolled removable tape under the flap.

Card 142 Christmas tree ✸✸

See template on page 110. Resize to suit.

Fold your cardstock in half. Align template to the fold line and trace. Decorate as you wish. I have used 'clear' bauble stickers on plum cardstock mounted on foam.

Card 141

Card 142

Card 143 J R's Wallet ✸✸✸✸

This is a handy card if you are giving a gift of cash, tickets or a voucher. You can make it any size you want.

- Cut out the four template pieces using heavy paper or lightweight cardstock.
- I stitched the edges of the cover strip before I adhered it across the outside strip.
- Score and fold both the inside and outside pieces in half. Note that the inside is a tad smaller all round. This allows room in the pocket for your gifts. I inked the top of the inside piece.
- Align the pieces at the bottom and both sides and attach with double sided tape. Only use a small amount on the bottom edge.
- Round the top corners with a corner punch.
- Add the side pocket aligning to the outer edge. You can add several pockets taller and shorter as you wish.
- I have used a circle punch to shape the inside of the pockets and inked the edges.
- Decorate as you wish. I have used individual gold stickers for the initials.
- Insert business card size gift tags with your best wishes.

See template on page 111.

Card 144 New home ✸✸✸✸

NOTE: This is a trifold card. See template page 112.

- Cut your cardstock 300x150mm. (Half a 12x12)
- Score your two fold lines 100mm from each side.
- Fold the first back and the second forward and crease well.
- Transfer the base shape from the template to the front page.
- Transfer the shape again to the second page but position it 10mm up from the base. If you want a chimney, add it at this time.
- Transfer to the third page 20mm up from the base.
- Decorate as you wish. Be mindful of which side will face the front when folded.

Card 143

Wallet cards are perfect for gifts of money, tickets or vouchers

Welcome to your new home!

Welcome to your new home!

Card 144

71

Make your own shapes

Select any shape you like and design your own card. Look for shapes in children's books, magazines, computer clip art or chipboard shapes. Fold your cardstock and trace the shape onto the card. Make sure you have a solid area for the fold line. Shapes to try: Heart, star, gingerbread boy, leaf, shoe, bear. Where do I stop?

Draw by hand

Card 145 Grandpa's saw ✤

My husband received this 'saw' shaped card from our family for Father's day. It has been decorated with sticker dots and a metallic pen.

Use your computer

Your computer can assist in making professional templates.

Card 146 First birthday ✤✤

- Using you favourite program print out a chunky number '1' and enlarge it to about 130mm high and 100mm wide. Try various fonts. Here I used playbill in capitals. Whatever number or letter you are using, imagine cutting the shape into a card. You need some of the shape to align with your card spine.

- Size your numbers to the size of your folded cardstock.

- Print this onto scrap paper, cut it out as a template and trace onto your cardstock.

- Using the same template trace the shape onto your decorative paper. When cutting this piece out, cut about 2mm inside the template to create a border all around.

- Decorate as you wish.

No computer? Draw your own shapes freehand

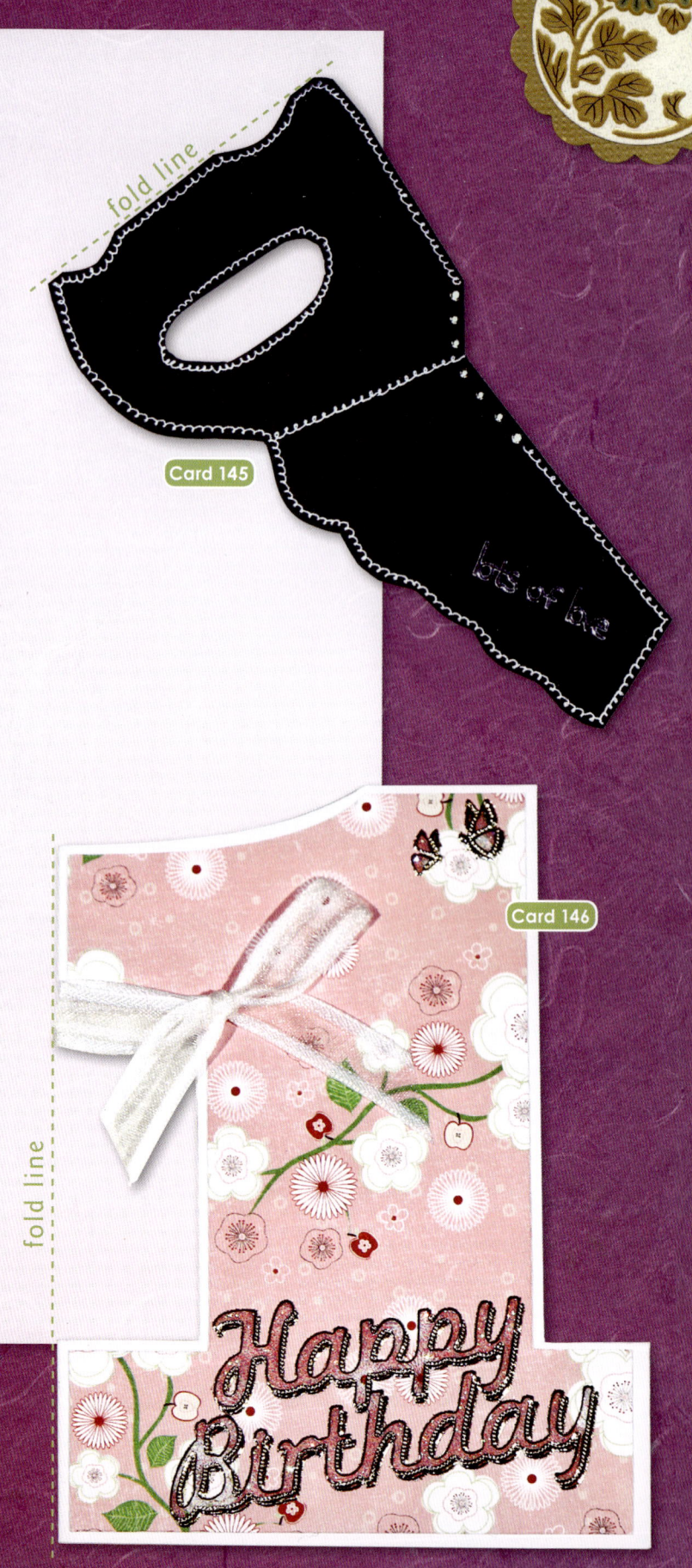

TIP: You could print out the individual letters, cut them out and arrange them overlapping each other to form a solid piece. Adhere them to your cardstock and cut around the full word.

Card 147 DB ✿✿

- Here I have printed two initials in playbill font.
- Using my publisher program I overlapped each letter to make a solid shape and still left a section to place on the fold line.
- I sized them to fit onto my card front.
- I coloured them to suit and printed them onto good quality paper.
- I cut them out and adhered them to my folded cardstock.
- I then cut through the entire card around the letter shapes.

Shapes as decoration

Geometric shapes

Card 148 It's a gift ✿

A small piece of beautiful Japanese paper cut into a square and tied up with gold twine. Mount it on a beautiful metallic print. Sends a very simple message and is a quick and easy card.

Card 149 Christmas triangle ✿

Cut a basic triangle shape using two different papers. Add some sticker decoration. Mount onto your card.

Card 150 Christmas triangle II ✿

Cut a triangle from Japanese paper and divide it into three pieces. Mount it on a triangle background. Layer it to your card.

Card 151 Welcome little one ✿✿

This is a notelet style card. See page 58. The caterpillar is made up from punched circles. The feelers and legs are actually petals from a punched daisy.

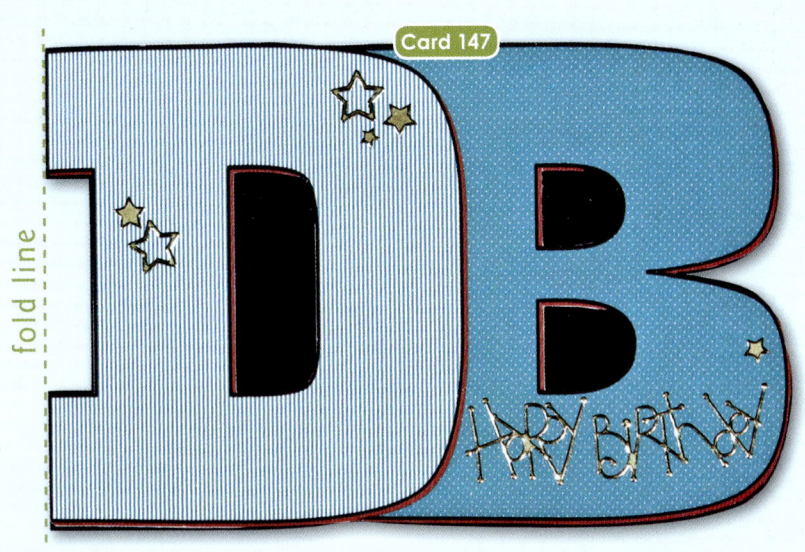

Appliqué patterns

Appliqué books and online patterns can yield suitable shapes to make up in paper. Google 'appliqué patterns'.

Card 152 Christmas time ✱

This was taken from an appliqué idea. A simple tree pattern decorated with buttons.

Card 153 My two girls ✱✱✱✱

I found these two little girls amongst my sewing paraphernalia. I enlarged and copied the picture. I cut out the dresses and various elements in suitable colour paper and arranged them on my background sheet. The hair is wound embroidery cotton. I machine stitched the background in blanket stitch. All the stitching on the girls themselves is done with an ink pen, as are their facial features.

Card 154 Silent night ✱✱✱✱

Though an appliqué design, I actually found this on a Christmas card I had received. I cut out the elements in various papers and arranged them roughly following their design. It was a little fiddly but I really enjoyed putting it together. I have not given you a template here. Just give it your own style.

Original pattern for Card 153

Card 152

Original greeting card

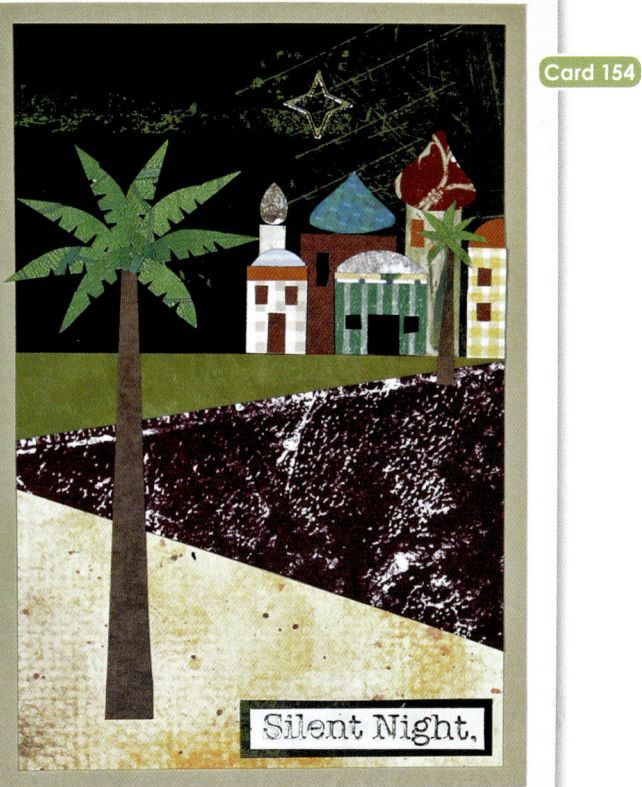

Card 154

Inspiration can come from many items found in your home

Card 153

75

Computer clip art

Many clip art pictures can be adapted for your cards.

Card 155 Easter bonnet ✦✦✦✦

I printed out this clip art rabbit shape and added a hat. I then cut out the pieces in various papers. I decorated the outfit with my flower punches. Marker pens added a face and gel pens highlighted the flowers.

Magazine pictures

Trace figures from magazines and dress them with paper.

Card 156 Beautiful Tara ✦✦✦✦

I cut out the entire shape of the girl and the dress in skin colour light cardstock. I pencilled in the chin and arm lines.

I cut out the hair and dress in suitable papers and adhered. I made the bow from a strip of silk paper but a ribbon would do.

Make your own pictures

Card 157 Très chic ✦✦

Cut flowers out of papers and build up your own picture. These beautiful cherry blossoms were on a 12x12 sheet.

I have raised them on foam. The stem I drew freehand on black paper and cut out. The vase is simple lines and mounted on foam.

Pictures from handmade papers

I refer to very soft fibre papers such as Japanese mulberry. Any papers that tear to give a lovely feathered edge.

Card 158 Paper daisies ✦✦

This is very much a freeform picture. I have torn circle shapes and tiny centre pieces for the flowers and rolled some papers for my stems. I used PVA glue diluted with a little water to adhere the pieces.

Card 159 Sweet peas ✦✦✦✦

If you want to get even more precise, copy a picture onto paper and cut out the individual pieces for a pattern.

Sit them on your mulberry paper and run a wet line around your pattern piece. See note on page 77.

Children's books are good source of cute animal pictures

NOTE: To tear these papers, dip a thin paintbrush in water and 'draw' the shape you want with a wet line. Then tear out the piece. Leave to dry. This will not take long.

Card 158

Card 157

Card 159

tres chic

77

Using up scraps

Little bits of paper

I save all my little bits of paper. They can always be used as a background or in a collage. Weave your off cut strips to form a mat. These are all the little strips left over when you trim a card or paper. Or punch your scrap pieces to create a background layer.

Card 160 Laughter ✶✶

Align two off cut strips in an 'L' shape on your mat and glue them at the corner. These are your anchor strips. Weave strips randomly, gluing them to the anchor strips and using your mat to keep them evenly spread and parallel. When you are happy with the effect, trim the mat to fit your card and find a suitable item to finish off. I added some rub on wording.

Card 161 Snow bird ✶✶

Small scraps of coordinating papers can be punched and combined for a background. I have used my 1" square punch to use up 3 scraps of coordinating paper. I stitched them in place and added a die-cut felt bird.

Card 162 My filigree heart ✶✶

I cut small scraps of coordinating papers with my flower punch. I centred a felt heart and spread the flowers over the rest of the paper. I trimmed any flowers overhanging the paper edge. I added a rhinestone to each flower and my rub on message.

TIP: You could use beads instead of the rhinestones to decorate the flower centres.

Collage

A form of abstract art in which photographs, pieces of paper etc are glued to the pictorial surface.

Also a great way to use up all those little bits of just about anything.

Card 163 Collage ✶✶✶✶

I start with my background layer. In this case the sky blue. Collect an assortment of elements and just see what happens! Build up layers, overlay small pieces, tear edges. When you have something you are happy with adhere it into place. Keep adding flowers, beads, lace, wording until you like the overall effect. Lastly select a suitable cardstock to mount it on.

TIP: You could give your collage a theme by selecting specific items that compliment each other.

Scraps can even be used to make embellishments.

78

TIP: Make your background, then find something suitable to put on it. I have had this white felt bird for sometime now, but suddenly this was the right background for it.

Card 163

Card 161

Card 162

May your day be filled with joy.

79

Stitching on cards

Stitching gives your cards a very interesting effect and another dimension to your work. You will get a definite right and wrong side so work on a layer, not on the actual card, then you can hide the back. You can hand stitch or use a machine. I am by no means a sewer. So for machine stitching I have one roll of off-white strong thread with a bobbin to match and almost all the machine stitching I do on cards is done with this thread. I know this colour tones with everything. The thread never causes me any grief and the machine is ready to go whenever I want to add stitching.

BUT. If you like hand stitching or machining and want to experiment with lots of varying threads and stitches, what a world awaits you.

Card 164 Jane's wallet ✦✦✦✦

For making a wallet see Card 143. This one is a bit bigger.

- I have used a strip of patterned paper for the outside 280x90mm.
- I cut a plain strip of light card 280x20mm and stitched the edges.
- I adhered this strip across the outside.
- The name is individual gold stickers.
- The main pocket inside was cut from light cardstock 270x80mm.
- I rounded the top corners with my corner punch and added an inside pocket.

TIP: To start stitching, tape the end of the thread to the back of your card. Once you have completed your stitching, again draw the thread ends to the back of the card and tape. There is no need to make bumpy knots to tie off your work.

Card 165 Daisy 'love' ✦✦✦✦

For this card I have used hand stitching of basic embroidery stitches using embroidery threads. Mark the stitch spacing with a pencil and ruler first to keep it even.

Card 166 Beaded flowers ★★★★

Beads and coloured threads make an easy decoration on a card. Use multicolour or metallic threads.

Copy the template from page 113 onto trace paper.

- Cut the layer of cardstock you will be stitching through to fit your card front.
- Lay the pattern over this layer and prick all the holes for your stitching. Use removable tape to hold your pattern in place.
- Tape the end of your thread to the back of the card and draw the thread up at point A. Go down at B, up at C, thread your beads and go down at B ready to come up again at A. I have used seed beads and rice beads. Bugle beads are also useful.
- Repeat until all the stitching is finished.
- Tape the end of the thread at the back when finished.
- Cover point A with your decoration item. Here I have used a paper tole picture.
- Then adhere the entire stitched layer to your actual card.

Card 167 Lace collage ★★★★

Stitching adds a good effect in collage cards. See page 78 for collage cards. This is very simple layering, machine stitched in place. I have wrapped a lace and ribbon strip around the layers. My floral disc is a round sticker inside a black rub on. I have added a few pearls and mounted the lot on foam.

Card 168 Aussie eucalypts ★★★★

Use stitching to attach unusual items. Here I have made a background of mixed paper pieces. I have adhered two real gum leaves and added machine stitching in a silky gold thread. I have also tied a small twig on with threads.

Card 167

Card 168

Card 166

81

Chapter 7 ✤ Give your cards dimension

These are cards that one way or another will have a 3 dimensional effect by either the fold or the decoration.

Some of these will be beyond the quick and easy and maybe a challenge for you.

Shaker cards

These are fun cards with a window full of something that moves when shaken. Glitter, sprinkles, sand, little beads, punched shapes. Whatever you wish to use. The windows can be any shape you choose.

NOTE: You do not need a huge amount of material under the window. It needs room to move so less is best.

Card 169 Fairy garden ✦✦✦✦

- Form your actual card and then cut the front layer for your window from cardstock. Mine is a standard A5 card with a 140x100mm layer.
- Cut a window in this layer. I used my large circle punch for the window.
- Ink the window edge and the other edges if you like.
- Cut a piece of clear acetate and adhere it to the back of the window. Double sided tape is fine.
- Select a background picture to put behind your window and adhere this to your actual card.
- You need to raise the window layer off the background to create a space for the shaker material to move in. You need to contain the material completely or it will fall out. Using mounting foam, cut strips to go around the inside of your window butting each piece to the next so there are no gaps. Add more foam to the edges of this layer so it is elevated the same height all across the card. Remember to support the corners. You do not need so much foam on the edges. Just enough to hold the whole layer in position.
- Mound your shaker material on top of your background picture where the window will sit.
- I have used about half a teaspoon of star scatters. Try to keep it in a small area.
- Now position the window overlay onto the card front enclosing the shaker material.
- Decorate as desired.

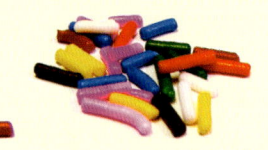

Card 169

Shaker window

Adhere acetate to the inside of your window.

Completely surround the window with foam tape and add more to the outer edges of the full layer.

Mound your shaker material under the window and cover with the top layer.

Card 170 Flower shake ✦✦✦✦

For this window I have punched a flower shape in patterned cardstock and then cut it out with my large circle punch.

I have backed the window with acetate and built it up with foam as above. My shaker material is punched small flowers.

More flowers complete the decoration.

Card 170

83

Stand-up cards

This style can be made any size. Just start with a square piece of cardstock. These make good place cards.

Card 171 Coralina ★★★★

- Start this card with a 140x140mm square cardstock.
- On the back draw a faint pencil line across the centre and 40mm above the centre.
- Measure in 30mm from each side and complete the rectangle. See diagram 171.
- Cut the 3 lines as shown in the diagram.
- Fold the card in half but do not fold the middle piece you just cut out.
- I have decorated the front 80mm square area so formed with a paper tole twisted pyramid design.

See page 53 for paper tole pyramids.

Card 172 Butterfly best wishes ★★★★

- Start this card with a 120x120mm square cardstock.
- Draw a line across the centre and find the mid point of this line. See diagram 172.
- Using your compass cutter and with radius 40mm cut half a circle on one side only of the centre line.
- Fold the card in half along this centre line but do not fold the circle area now formed.
- Cut mats of decorative papers with your circle cutter.
- I have used a 3D butterfly sticker to decorate. See page 45 for this butterfly.

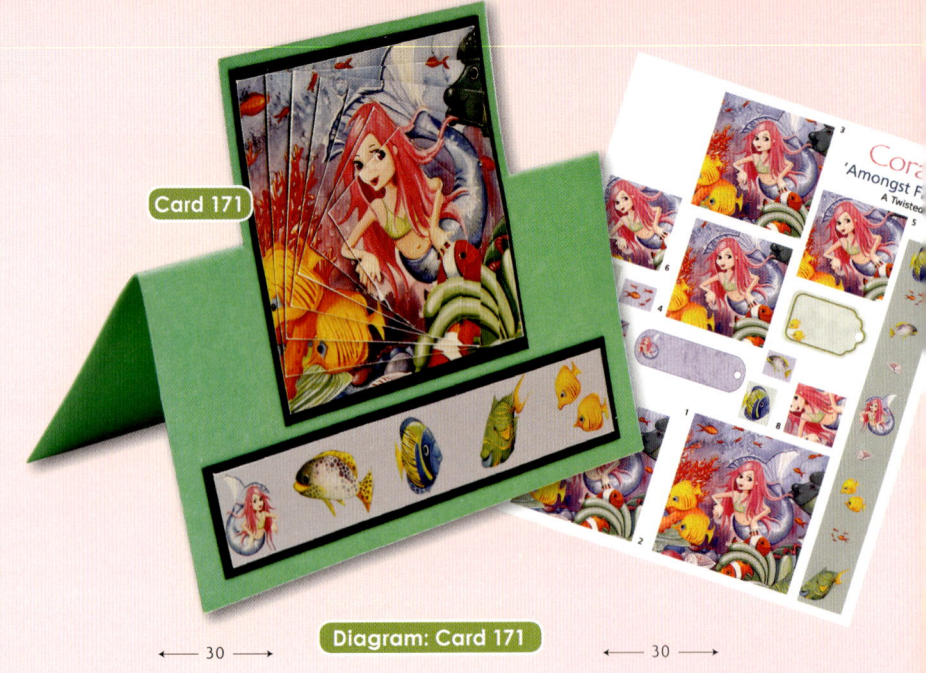

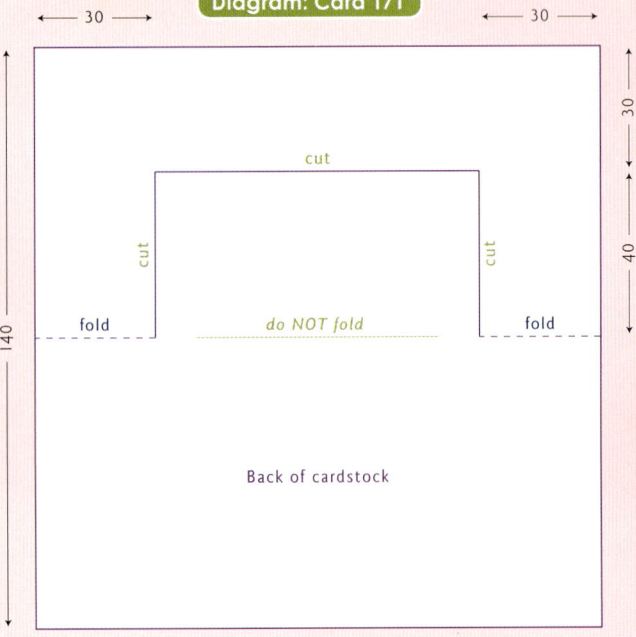

Diagram: Card 171

(140mm square; 30mm in from each side, 40mm tall rectangle from fold; cut top and sides, do NOT fold middle, fold sides)

Diagram: Card 172

(120mm square; half circle radius 40mm on fold line; cut the arc, do NOT fold the circle area, fold sides)

Spring cards

A spring card is just that. It springs up when you sit it on the mantelpiece. You can make them any size but be mindful as always of the folded size for finding an envelope to fit.

Card 173 I Do ✦✦✦✦

- Start with cardstock 240x120mm. This will fit in a 130mm square envelope.
- On the back mark lines across this card at 60mm, 120mm and 180mm.
- Mark the diagonals of the centre section and the centre point X.
- Mark the mid point of the top and cut off the two corners. See diagram 173.
- Mountain fold the 2 lines across the card.
- Valley fold the 2 diagonals.
- Turn the card over and push the centre of the card X toward you forming a peak. You should be able to pull that peak right down onto the base.
- Decorate the front diamond shaped section.
- Put a piece of double sided tape in the middle of the base and pull the centre section down onto the tape.
- Decorate the two triangular sections now showing on the base.
- This card will fit into a square envelope 130x130mm. Decorate it to match.

Diagram: Card 173

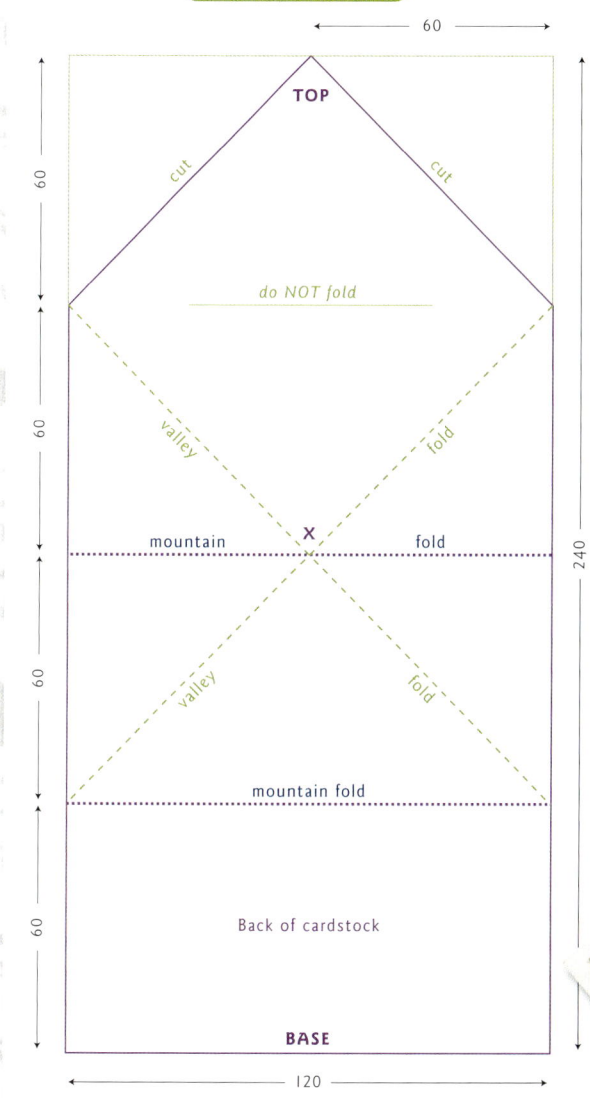

Draw on back of cardstock

85

Paper flowers

These are very easy flowers to make. I have used handmade Nepalese papers for this colourful card but any soft papers including crepe paper work well. These flower bunches go well on boxes. For cards they are not exactly post friendly!

Card 174 Burst of colour ✸✸✸✸

- On your choice of paper draw a rough petal shape with a bit of a stem. See image. They do not have to be exact nor all perfectly the same.
- I have stitched around the coloured ones but that is not essential. Crepe papers tend to stretch when stitched.
- Cut out the individual petals. I find you need at least five for a flower.
- Give each petal a soft pleat in the centre and bind the stem area with cotton thread or tape.
- Repeat for all petals.
- Holding their stems, group them together and tie or tape them tight to form your flower.
- Once you have them secured you can shape them and then cut away most of the stem.
- I used two more 'petals' for leaves in my coloured bunch and added beads to their centre.

NOTE: The single white flower was made using crepe paper. I inked the edges, put a drop of PVA glue in the centre and sprinkled in tiny beads.

Card 174

Pop-up cards

I love making pop-up cards. They are not exactly quick and easy but a lot of fun.

Concertina pop-up

This is the easiest to make but does require a longer than usual piece of cardstock.

Card 175
Seasons greetings ★★★★

- Cut two pieces of cardstock both 140mm wide. One is 250mm long and the other 180mm. If you have cardstock that is 420mm wide, turn to page 113 for diagram.
- Score and fold the longer piece at 90mm and 180mm.
- Score and fold the shorter piece at 50mm, 100mm and 170mm.
- Fit them together in a concertina and join with the 10mm strip overlapping using double-sided tape.
- It is now just a matter of your choice of decoration.

I have used recycled cards and stickers. Mine are flat but you can lift some items with foam. You can ink the edges of course. Let things go above the folds and out off the sides. Keep closing the card to see the effect before you actually glue things down.

Don't forget to make it fit your envelope! Have fun!

Diagram: Card 175a

Diagram: Card 176

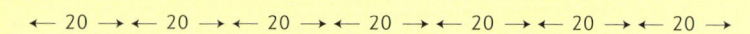

Pop-up inserts

Most pop-up cards rely on the insert to support the pop-up items.

Card 176 Surprise ★★★★

- Fold A5 cardstock and decorate the front.
- Cut an insert 140x200mm using a slightly heavier paper than usual.
- Following diagram 176 faintly pencil mark inside your insert and cut where indicated.
- Fold as indicated and erase pencil marks.
- Attach your insert to your card in the same way as described on page 15.
- The inside will now 'pop up' when you open the card.
- Decorate the inside of the card using the fronts of the pop-up sections to support your items. I have used flower punches with rhinestone centres, a small butterfly sticker and a rub on for the wording.

Have fun!

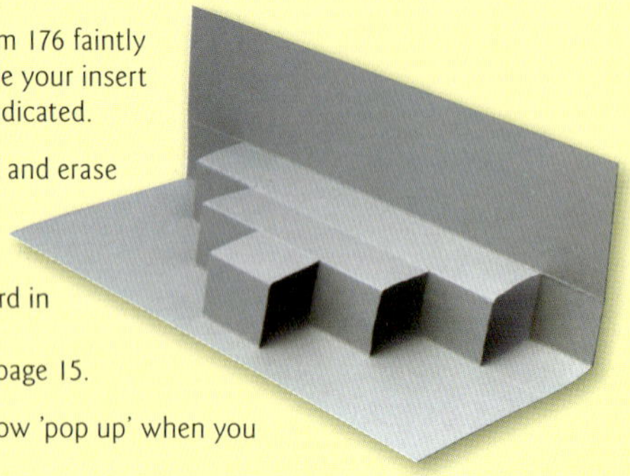

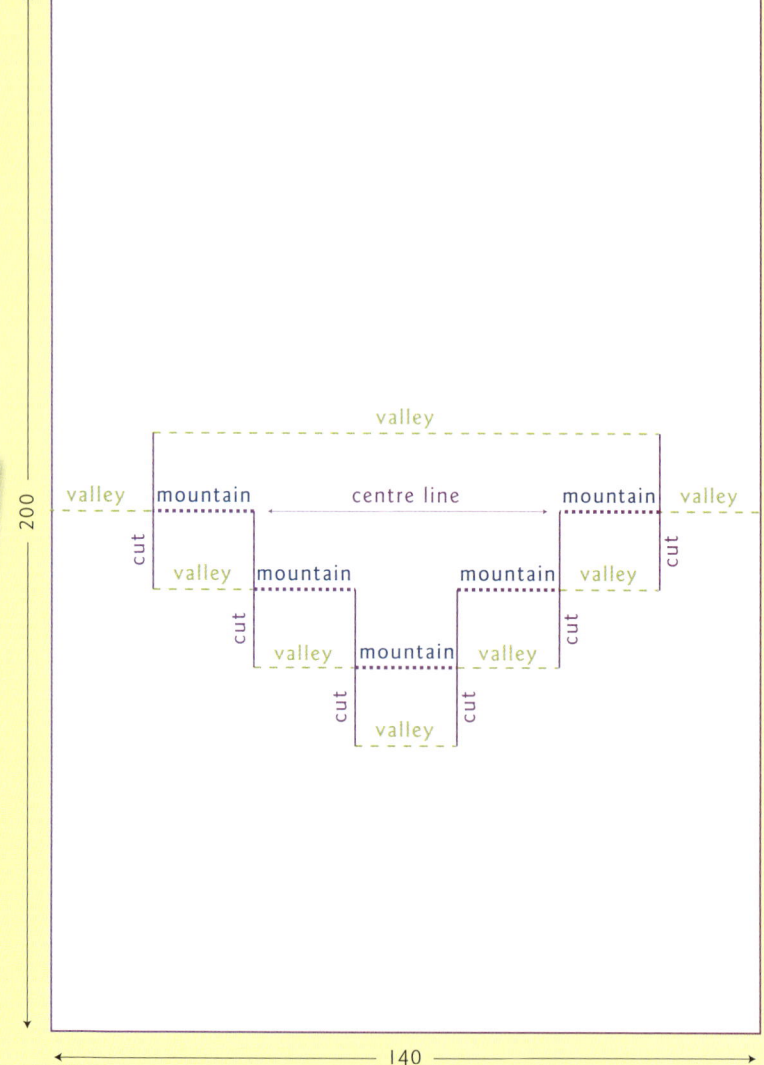

Card 177 Rayna's flower pot ★★★★

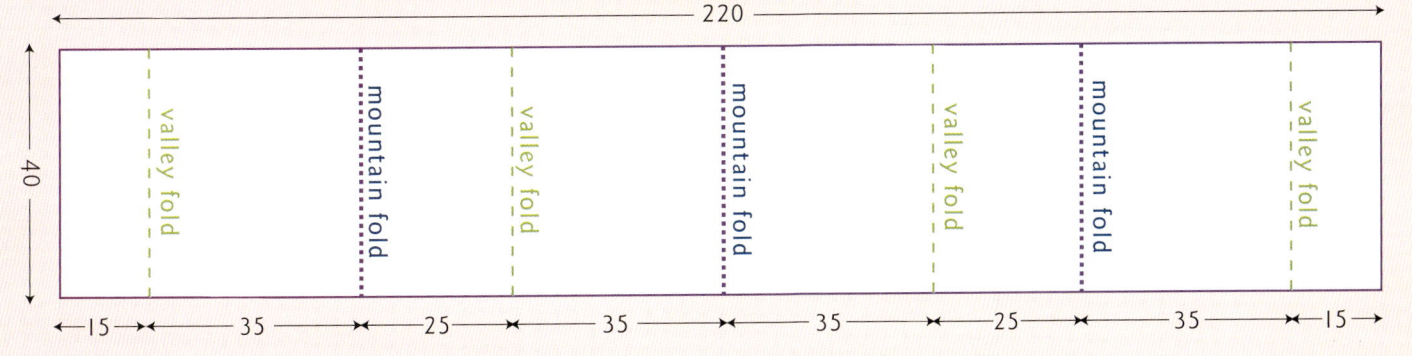

This little flower pot or vase has a full bunch of flowers inside.

- I have used a flocked cardstock but corrugated card also works well for this card.
- Using the template on page 114 cut out the pot shape and fold in half.
- Cut a strip 20mm off the top front and back. Turn these strips down on the card to form the pot rim.
- Select a light card or heavy paper for the inside mechanism. Cut a strip 40mm wide and 220mm long.
- Score and concertina fold at the measurements marked in diagram 177.
- The two short flaps at either end are the hinges. Attach these inside the pot to the front and back near the base.
- With your pot facing you decorate the front of each section of the concertina and inside the card back. Four sections altogether.
- Decorate the front on the outside.
- Add a ribbon tie. Attach it on the back with double sided tape.

Notes on decorating your pot:

Before adding a decoration, hold it in place and close the card to check if it is concealed.

I made strips 10mm wide as stalks for my flowers. I then stuck the stalk to the concertina strip.

Diagram: Card 177 Insert

220 × 40

valley fold — mountain fold — valley fold — mountain fold — valley fold — mountain fold — valley fold

15 — 35 — 25 — 35 — 35 — 25 — 35 — 15

Exploding cards

This is just a different fold for the inside pages of your card or book. For this you will need boxboard or heavy cardboard for the front and back, decorative papers to cover the front and back and lightweight cardstock for the inside pages.

Card 178
Grandma's little darling! ✹✹✹✹

Cut boxboard or heavy cardboard 100x100mm.

- Cut two decorative papers 150x150mm and cover the cardboard pieces just like covering a school book. I actually put PVA glue on the entire front cover. Mitre the corners, fold in and glue to secure.
- Cut a ribbon tie and attach it across the centre of the back cover on the inside with double sided tape.
- For the pages cut three sheets of light cardstock 180x180mm. I used different colours for mine.
- Score each sheet in half horizontally and vertically and fold to get sharp creases.
- Open out each sheet, turn over and score one diagonal only. Fold and crease.
- Assemble the three pieces with the smooth quarters in a line as per diagram 178 and the diagonals folds alternating mountain, valley, mountain.
- Glue securely the two pairs of overlapping quarters with the shaded quarters on top.
- Decorate as you like but be mindful of how the page will open to align photos correctly.
- Fold up completely and attach back cover to the back of square 2 and the front cover to the back of square 1.
- Take care that the ribbon is aligned to fold over.

Notes on decorating:

Photos work well in these albums. Cut photos to 70x70mm and add to a layer 80x80mm. Adhere to the smooth panels.

Decorate the folding panels with triangular pieces. Maybe include journaling.

Card 179 Poppy post ✹✹✹✹

Put together in the same way as above though smaller dimensions.

Covers are 300gsm coloured cardstock 72x72mm.

The inside pages are140x140mm. I used 120gsm papers for the pages. The smaller the album, the lighter you can go with the covers and the pages.

NOTE: If you chose to make this a bit smaller or did not want to mount heavy photos on the inside papers you could make it with cardstock covers and paper for the inside pages.

Card 179

Card 179

Diagram: Card 178

Back Cover
Square 2
Ribbon tie on back

Photo orientation

'valley' folds
'mountain' folds

Square 1
Front Cover

91

Star cards

These are lovely cards to share or display a number of photos. I make one up for each holiday we take. I fit sixteen photos in them, the highlights of our trip. Make them up for any situation where you need multiple pages to tell your story.

Card 180
The colours of Alaska ★★★★

A star card is actually a combination of several cards with multi inserts. You need at least seven and you can make these the dimensions of your choice. The number of folios will vary according to the size of the card.

- I have made this star card with a finished size of 140x140mm.
- I cut seven cardstock of the same colour 280x140mm, seven light card of a second colour 210x139mm and seven light card of a third colour 190x139mm.
- I scored and folded all in half.
- Now make up seven individual folios each with the three sizes biggest to smallest.
- The smallest insert is the one you will be decorating and it is easier to do this before you join the folios together. You will be decorating the inside of the folio.
- Adhere these three sections together at the outer edges with a full run of double sided tape.
- Now adhere these seven folios in order by taping the back of one to the front of the next.
- To finish, run ribbon around the card from front to back to hold it all together.
- Cover the ribbon with a layer of decoration front and back if you wish.

Card 181
Cherry blossom time ★★★★

Done in exactly the same way as 180.

Card 182
Mother Nature's garden ★★★★

For this star card I used four pages per folio and had a total of seven folios. My smallest page was a series of garden pictures. Remember to fold the picture in. You decorate the inside of the smallest page.

- My outer cardstock was 240x85mm.
- My inner paperweight folios were 200x83mm, 170x83mm and 140x83mm.
- I decorated the front panel only with handmade paper and left the ribbon tie on the outside.

NOTE: I made the inside pieces of each folio 1mm narrower than the outside so they sit right down inside. Try to use the strongest cardstock on the outside but lighter pieces inside or it will all become too bulky.

Star card folio

Here each folio has three folded sheets decreasing in width. Make sure you keep any patterns or pictures all up the same way.

Join the three pages together at the outer edges with double-sided tape.

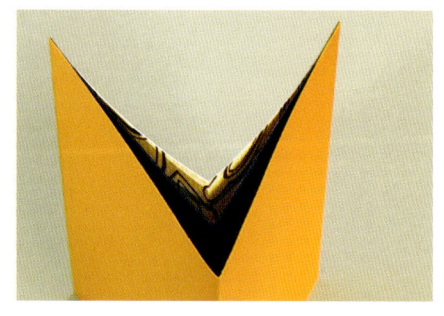

Once all folios are made up, adhere the back of the first one to the front of the second and so on.

Card 183

Card 182

Card 183 Star decoration ✸✸✸✸

This is a very tiny star card with three pages per folio and eight folios. Due to the tiny size I used a glue stick for all the adhering rather than tape to cut down on bulk.

- My outer cardstock was 80x21mm.
- My inner paperweight folios were 60x20mm and 40x20mm.
- The innermost folio was a lovely metallic paper so no need for any further decoration.
- I simply tied this with ribbon.

Card 181

93

Trick cards

I just love quirky folds and the following two are my favourites.

Trick Card 1

This card is fun as it opens not once but twice. This has many possibilities to trick the recipient.

Card 184
Pussy cat, pussy cat ✦✦✦✦

This card is made out of all the one colour cardstock with no background papers.

- Cut your card stock to A5. You will also need two more strips 150x52mm.

- Mountain fold the A5 piece in half, then fold both sides back to the centre fold.

- Open out again and align your card on your mat. Cut two slits across the card from each side fold, 50mm from the top and bottom of the card. See diagram Trick Card 1.

- Using the other two strips, weave the first one under the card centre and the second strip over the card centre. They should fit snugly in the centre of the card and hold each other in place. Trim them if necessary or cut them again a tad bigger if they are too loose and falling out.

- Now close your card as a centre opening card.

- Open to the first page as normal.

- Concertina the centre fold up toward you and open the centre to reveal the second page.

- Decorate your card.

Notes on decorating

The easiest way to decorate this card is with individual items such as these cats. These are all either stickers or die-cut chipboard. Open each page and decorate as one full sheet. Just make sure each item is entirely on the one square panel. Do not have anything overlapping the edges or folds where the card pivots from one page to the next.

Diagram: Trick Card 1

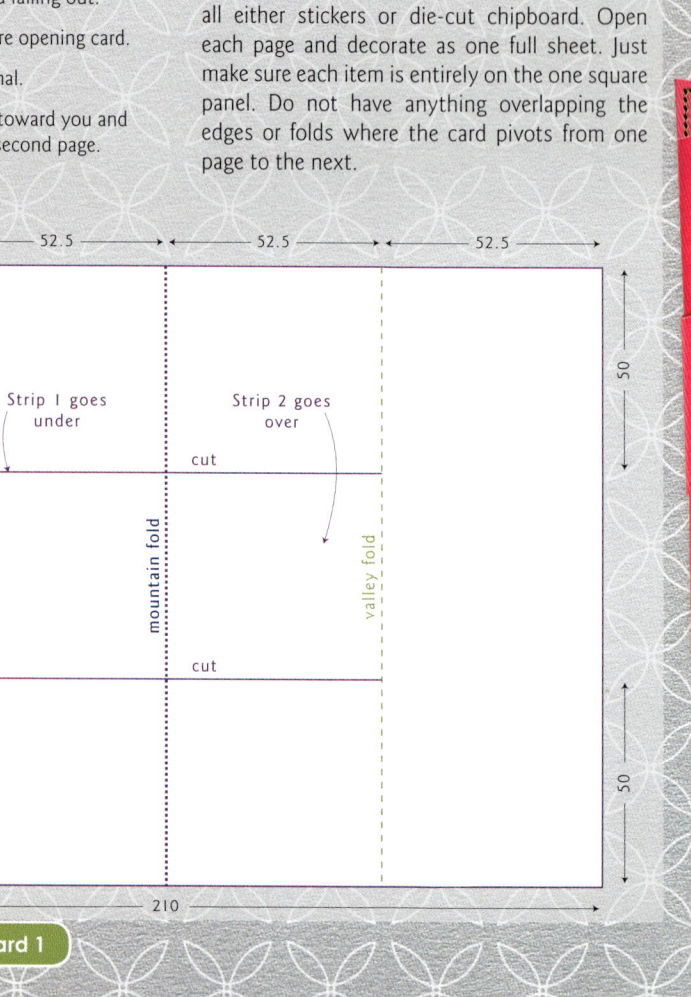

Card 185 Beary funny! ★★★★

This card is made in the same way as card 184 but I have used a decorative paper as a background on each page.

- Cut your cardstock and strips as above and put the basic card together as for card 184.
- Select your background papers. Try to avoid patterns that must be aligned perfectly such as checks or lines. I chose a pattern that is somewhat random.
- Select your full background for the first page inside. (150x200mm). This is the central part of your card, not the side panels. Cut this piece into squares that fit on each of the sections of the centre strips. Each square is a tad under 50x50mm. Depending on your pattern, make sure you know which is the top of each piece and which is left and right.
- Adhere the squares to page one in order. You are actually sticking some to the card and some to the strips.
- Add wording if desired. See note below.
- Now open page two. Repeat this process.
- Decorate the fronts and inside fronts if desired.

Note on wording
If adding wording do not cross over the folds or edges of the square panels. I printed the words on my computer then cut them out individually. Keep each word entirely on the one square panel.

95

Trick card 2

This card is essentially a flat card but folds through four different positions. I first encountered it as a business card but have adapted the fold for fun greeting cards. I make mine about postcard size.

Card 186 Happy birthday ★★★★

This card is cut from two coordinating 12x12 sheets. I have inked the edges on each page with gold. Decorations are simple stickers.

Card 187 Good luck! ★★★★

Again I use 12x12 papers. I have used a marker pen to define each page and stickers.

Paper selection

You require a card front and a card back. I use heavy papers rather than cardstock. Choose two different papers each double-sided, even if one side is only a different colour. Complimentary papers from a 12x12 set are ideal.

It is much easier to decorate if the insides are not too busy. At one point the back will actually be upside down so avoid wording or papers with a definite one way up for the back. This is not a problem for the front. Cut your card front and card back each 140x100mm.

Card front

Determine which side of the paper will be the front. Working on the reverse side of this piece, lightly pencil in the lines as in diagram Trick Card 2 Front. Each side is divided into four even sections. Mark the numbers in the four corners as indicated. Fold the top and bottom into the middle, crease and open out. Then cut this piece through the centre vertically.

Card back

Determine which side of the paper will be the back of the card. Again, working on the reverse of this piece, mark the lines as in diagram Trick Card 2 Back. Each side is again divided into four even sections. Mark the numbers in the four corners as indicated. Fold the two sides into the centre, crease and open out. Then cut this piece through the centre horizontally.

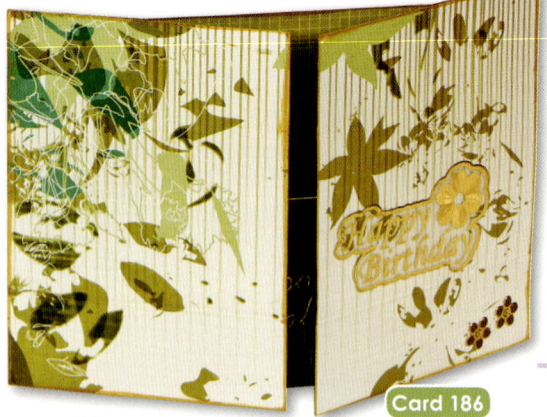

Assembly

Lay the two pieces of the back next to each other with the numbers showing. Apply glue to the four corner sections with the numbers 1 to 4 in them. Now turn the front onto the back matching the corners to the numbers. You are only gluing the four corners each to its respective number.

I have used a glue stick generously as you need the entire section held fast. Allow the glue to dry completely before trying to manipulate the card.

Decorating your card

Apart from the back which will be upside down at one stage, all the rest of the pages will be as you see them.

Avoid decorating across fold lines. I tend to stay in the middle area of each page.

Have fun with it!

Folding Sequence

1. Card front with centre opening.
2. Open the card at the centre and fold edges right back.
3. Fold the top up and the bottom down to form a cross shape.
4. Open the card from the centre right back. This will reveal the back of the card but it will be upside down.
5. Again fold the top up and the bottom down to return to the original card front.

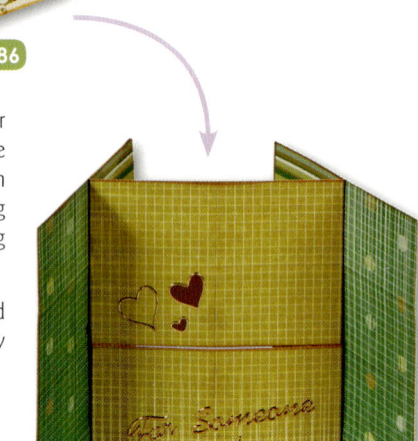

TIP: With both pieces make sure the fold lines are very sharp using your bone scorer and that they can fold back and forth.

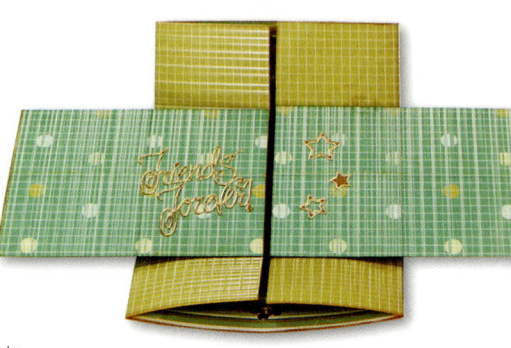

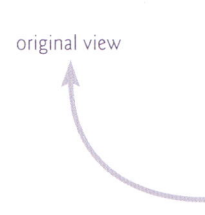

Card 186

original view

96

Card 187

Diagram: Trick Card 2 Front

glue 2	Draw on reverse side	glue 1
	fold ··· fold	
pencil	cut	pencil
	fold ··· fold	
glue 4		glue 3

100 | 140

Diagram: Trick Card 2 Back

glue 1	Draw on reverse side	glue 2
	pencil	
fold	cut	fold
fold	pencil	fold
glue 3		glue 4

25 | 25 | 25 | 25

35 | 35 | 35 | 35

original view

97

TIP: A very narrow box such as this silver one looks excellent as a decoration and can be embellished as such. Ideal to pop in a voucher or money gift.

Chapter 8 ✸ Beyond cards

Boxes

There are lots of box templates available free online to download. Just google 'box templates free.' However, some of them are very fiddly or tricky to get a professional finish.

These would have to be my favourite boxes. Quick and easy.

Triangular box

This one is so easy and great to use up scrap pieces of cardstock or heavy paper. You can make this box from any rectangular piece. You can get long skinny boxes, short fat boxes, large or small depending on the shape of your rectangle. I have used heavy printed papers and cardstock. The bigger the box, the heavier the cardstock needs to be.

Box 1 White with green swirls ✸
Cut cardstock to 150x200mm.

Box 2 Lime with pink flower ✸
Cut cardstock to 120x300mm.

Box 3 Blue floral ✸
Cut cardstock to 80x120mm.

Box 4 Red with window ✸✸
Cut cardstock to 90x160mm.

Box 5 Blue and silver tree decoration ✸
Cut cardstock to 40x200mm. I have added a hanger to one end and strung beads on twine the other end.

Box 4

TIP: You can cut a window as I have done with Box 4. I have taped acetate to the back of the window.

These windows look very good if the box is filled with sweets or cookies.

Method for all triangle boxes

See diagram for Triangle Box

- Mark the midpoint of all four sides.
- Score across the centre, fold and crease well.
- Now score and fold from the edge of this crease to the centre of the other two sides.
- Fold the triangular sides in to form your box.
- Holding the two flaps on one side together and pushed in as far as they will go, punch a hole through both pieces together for your tie.
- Repeat on other side.
- Thread with ribbon and pull together.
- Decorate as required.

Diagram: Triangle Box 1

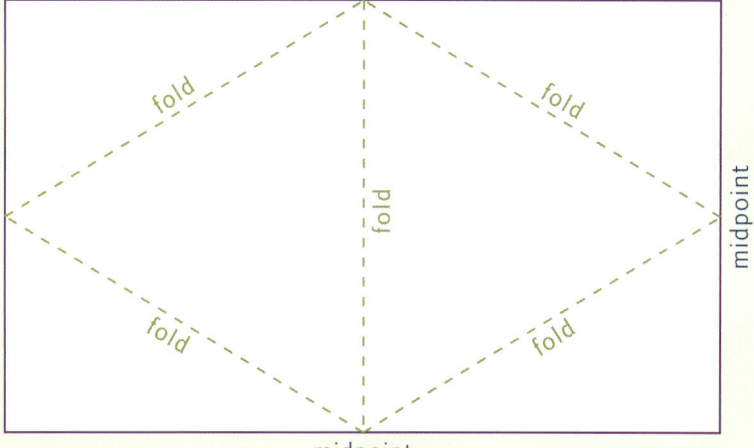

fold / fold / fold / fold / fold / midpoint / midpoint

Triangle boxes

Mark the midpoints of all sides. Score and fold as per diagram.

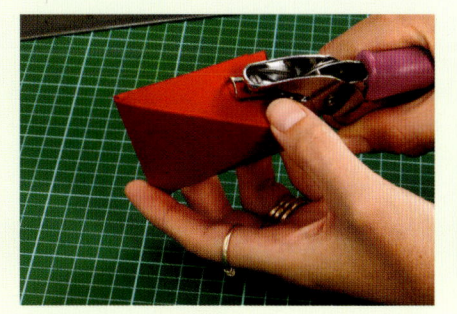

Fold up into a box shape.

Punch holes for your ribbon ties.

99

Puffy boxes

Again, very simple to make and can be made any size. I find these are easier if I use heavy paper rather then cardstock.

Box 6 White with black blossoms
Start with a rectangular paper piece 200x120mm.

Box 7 Pink gingham
Start with a rectangular paper piece 200x150mm.

Box 8 Blue check
Start with a rectangular paper piece 150x100mm.

TIP: Box 7 is held shut with a ribbon tie but I find they hold together better if sealed shut with tape.

Puffy boxes

Roll your paper into a short, fat cylinder and tape the ends where they overlap.

With this join in the middle, flatten one end just creasing the corners and tape this side closed.

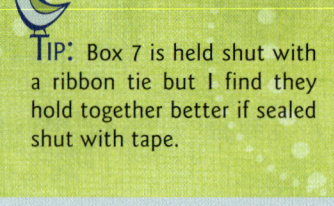

Holding this taped end vertical, flatten the other end at right angles to the first just creasing the corners. Fill the box before you tape it closed. Again, decorate as you wish.

TIP: Plastic laundry pegs are handy to hold a join in place while waiting for PVA glue to dry.

Pillow boxes

These have always been very popular boxes. There is a base template on page 109. Enlarge or reduce to suit.

If you want them longer, extend the central area. The arched flaps will still be the same.

Cardstock including corrugate is excellent for these boxes but for the tiny one I used printed metallic paper. (120gsm)

Box 9 White corrugate ✼✼

This box has a finished size 90x70mm. A simple ribbon tie is all I have used here.

Box 10 Natural corrugate ✼✼

Finished size 120x75mm. Lace is a nice alternative to ribbon. Add decorative items as you wish.

Box 11 Silver lace ✼

This tiny box is only 80x40mm. I have added a string of beads on top of the ribbon. They are threaded on fine jewellers' wire and tied at the back.

Method for all pillow boxes:

Cut out the template and trace it onto cardstock or heavy paper. Score all the fold lines firmly and crease. Fold the basic box shape and adhere the overlap with double sided tape or PVA glue. Fold in the arched flaps and secure with ribbon. Decorate as you wish.

101

Jacky box

This too is an easy box and no actual measuring required. Thank you Jacky.

Box 12 Christmas pinecones box ✻

I have used two 12x12 double sided prints. The box and lid inside and out all coordinate. See diagram for Jacky Box.

- Cut light cardstock into two rectangles the same size. Mine are 100x140mm.
- Trim the one you want for the bottom of the box about 5mm shorter than the other. Each piece is then folded in the same way.
- On the inside of your cardstock, using your ruler, lightly pencil in the diagonals to find the centre point of the rectangle.
- Fold each edge in as far as this centre mark and crease with your bone scorer.
- Flatten out and cut in from the edge at four positions as per diagram.
- Pull up to form a box shape folding in the corners and adhere to hold. If the ends are higher than the sides fold them over and down inside the box and adhere.
- Repeat with the other piece. One will be just a tad smaller to fit inside the other.
- Decorate as required.

TIP: Make sure your rectangles are actually exact rectangles. Often scraps are not quite what they seem.

Box 13 Christmas tree box ✻

Use a bought card for this box. Cut your card in half to give two rectangles the same size. When made up, the front of the card will form the lid and the message inside the card will be in the bottom of the box. Follow directions for box 12.

Box 14 Graduation box ✻

(See Card 130.)

Instead of a rectangle, make up as above using a square. I used cardstock 100x100mm for a finished box 50x50mm.

You may find no length to fold over on the sides but you can still secure the ends to form a box.

TIP: Use a small circle punch to take a semicircle nip out of box rims for ease of opening. Works well on the flaps of the pillow box too.

Box 12

Diagram: Jacky Box

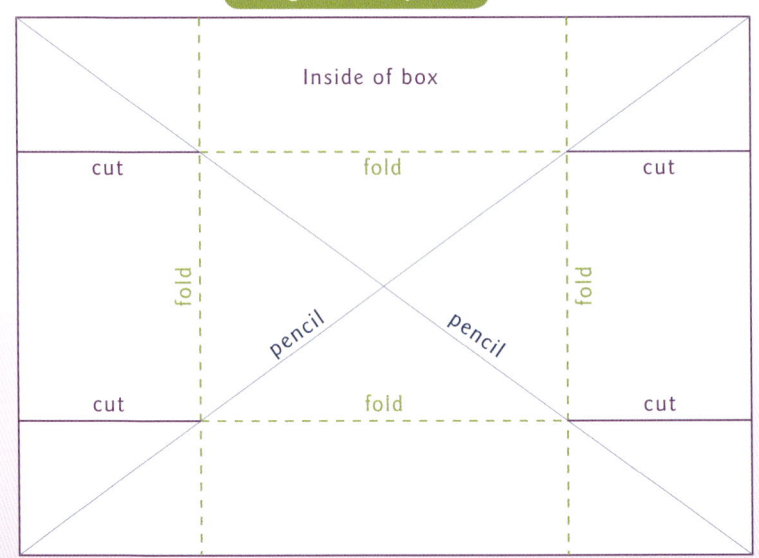

cut	fold	cut
fold	Inside of box / pencil	fold
cut	fold	cut

Box 13

Box 14

Decorating gift bags is a good way to use up leftover paper scraps

103

Gift wraps

Gift bags
Decorate your gift bags with papers and punches.

Paper bags
These are simple to create from your paper stock. Made in the same way as the sleeve for Card 140.

Gift wrap
Use your decorative papers to wrap little gift items such as soap. You can dress up an inexpensive but useful gift just by using a beautiful choice of paper and ribbons.

TIP: The music paper has been printed from the net. Google 'free sheet music'.

Decorations

Baubles

It is very easy to make baubles for your Christmas tree using your punches. Circles, squares, ovals (scalloped or plain) all work well.

- Punch the same shape at least six times out of decorative papers.
- Fold each shape in half, decorative side in and crease well. For square shapes, consider folding on the diagonal.
- With the pieces still folded in, join them together with a glue stick in a stack one on top of the other. Make sure they are very neatly aligned. Allow the glue to dry completely.
- When dry, spread the leaves out to form a bauble. You will still have two panels to glue together to hold the shape.
- Form a loop of ribbon or twine to use as a hanger. Make it extend out the bottom and thread beads on the ends if you wish.
- Position the hanger between the last two leaves right in the centre fold and glue with PVA.
- When the hanger is dry, glue the last two leaves together with the glue stick.

105

TIP: Wrapping paper is a good source of larger sheets of suitable paper for the envelope.

Envelope 1 See template on page 109
This is the envelope I used for Card 122. I made it 100mm across the centre but you can resize to suit.

Envelope 2
Select a piece of paper 30mm wider than your card and 2 ½ times longer. See diagram envelope 2.

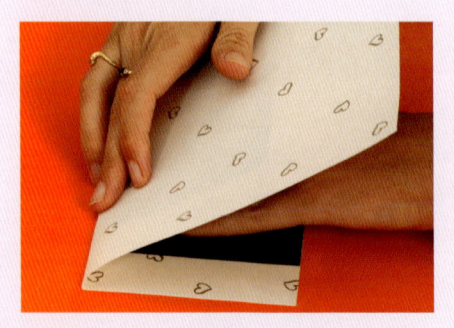

Easy envelopes

A few ideas on envelopes

I cannot stress enough to make a card to fit your envelope. I have known people to make eighty+ wedding invitations and then go out to buy their envelopes and not be able to find any suitable. Making 80 envelopes would be very tedious.

If making your own envelope remember that they actually can take a surprisingly large piece of paper. Often you require a piece bigger than the standard sizes available.

Decorate your envelope to tie in with the card. For weddings this really sets the theme right from the first glance.

NOTE: Leave a bit of room around the card so it will slip easily into the envelope.

With your card on the bottom of the paper fold the top of the paper down over the card and open up again.

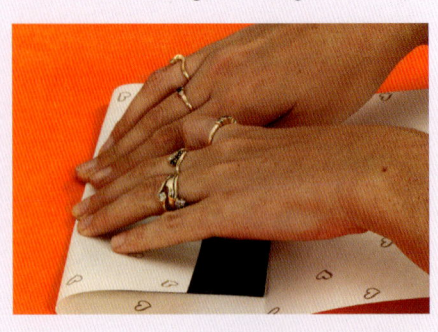

Now put your card on this fold line and again fold the top of the paper down and open up again.

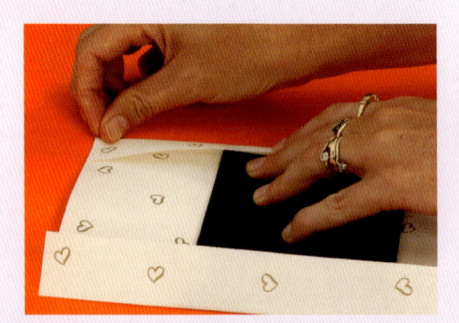

Centre your card and fold in the sides and open up again. Your paper will now look like step 2 on the diagram.

Now cut away the four corner sections and adhere the sides with double-sided tape.

Diagram: Envelope 2

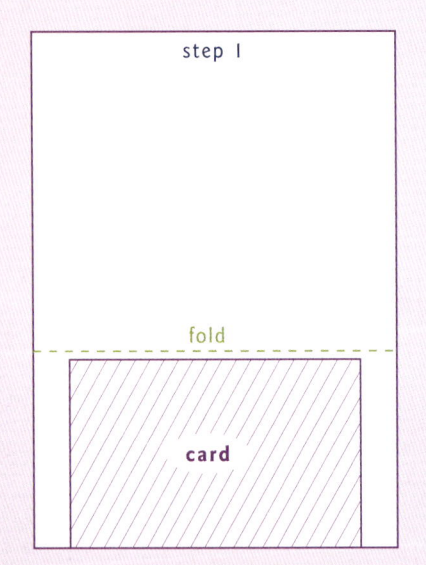

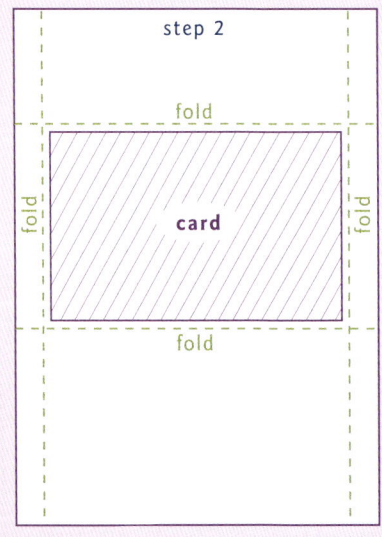

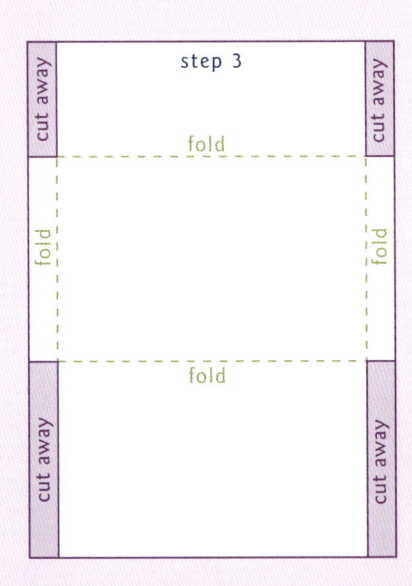

step 1 — card, fold

step 2 — fold, card, fold (all four sides)

step 3 — cut away (four corners), fold (all four sides)

106

Envelope 3

This envelope works well for squat cards.

Measure your card's diagonal, add 20mm and cut a square piece of paper this size.

Using the grid on your mat, sit the paper right side down on the diagonal and place your card centrally on the paper.

Now fold in the four sides using your mat gridlines to keep it square.

Adhere the base flap to the sides.

Trim any excess as necessary.

Envelope 2

Envelope 1

Envelope 3

107

Chapter 9 ✽ A little bit of help

Fonts

Search on the net for free fonts. Some of my favorite fonts are:

Alba Matter	Asenine	ARTISTAMP MEDIUM	CityBlueprint
Comic Sans MS	Courier New	Curlz MT	Edwardian Script
Freestyle Script	Harrington	Kristen ITC	Lucida Handwriting
Mistral	Papyrus	Playbill	Pristina
Rage Italic	Ravie	Scriptina	Tempus Sans

Templates

Pillow Box – Resize to suit

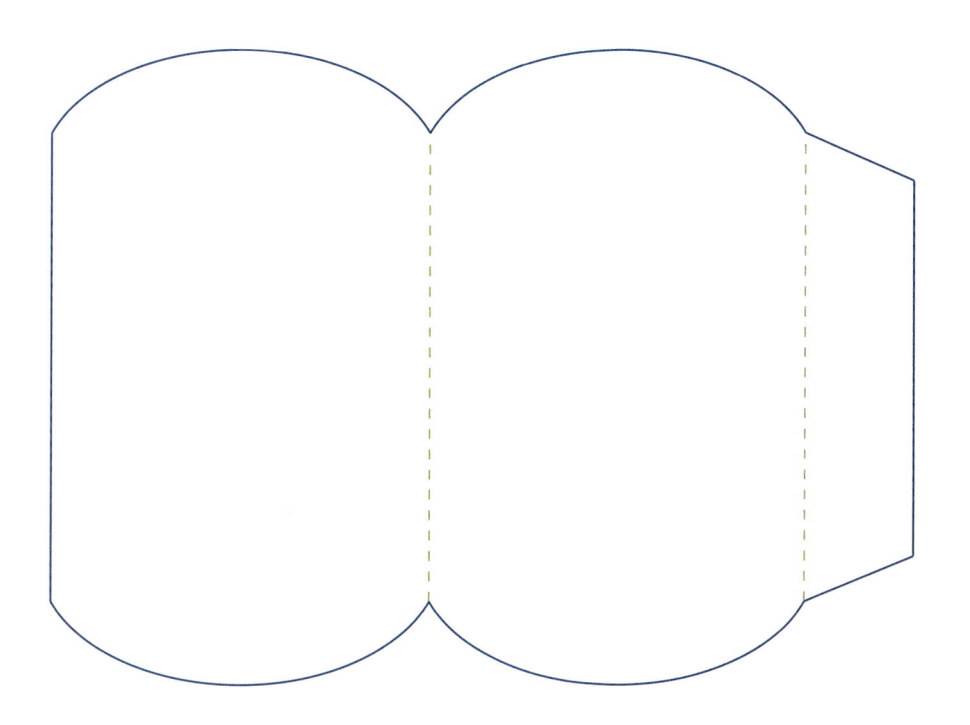

Basic Envelope – Resize to suit

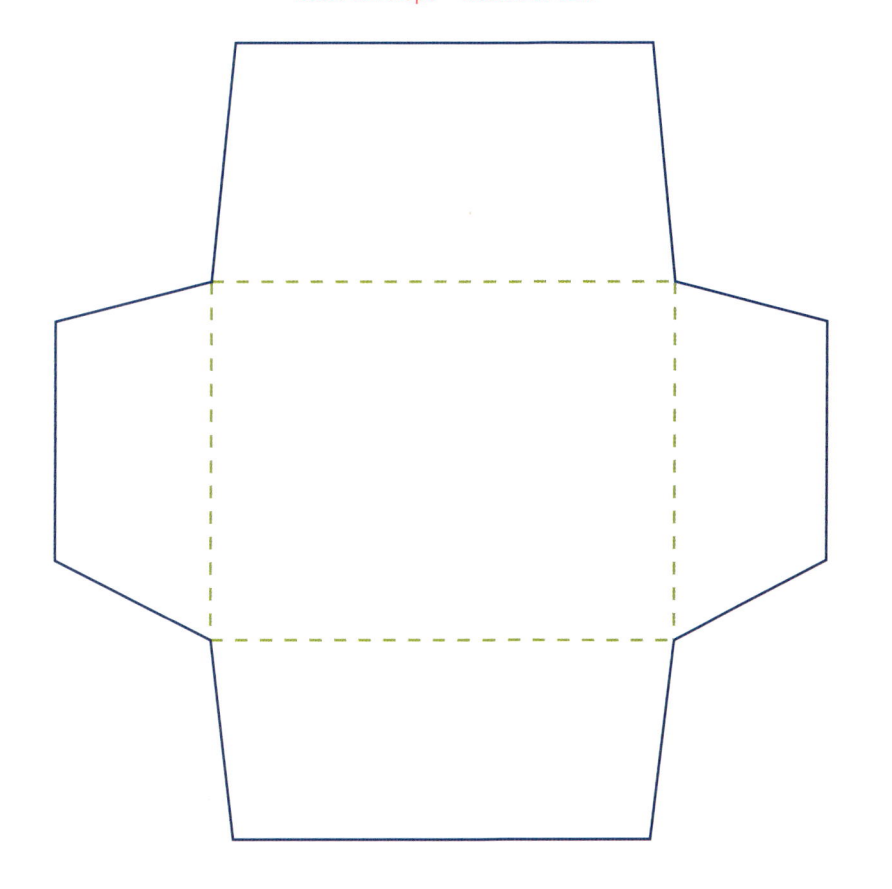

Card 141 – Handbag – Actual size

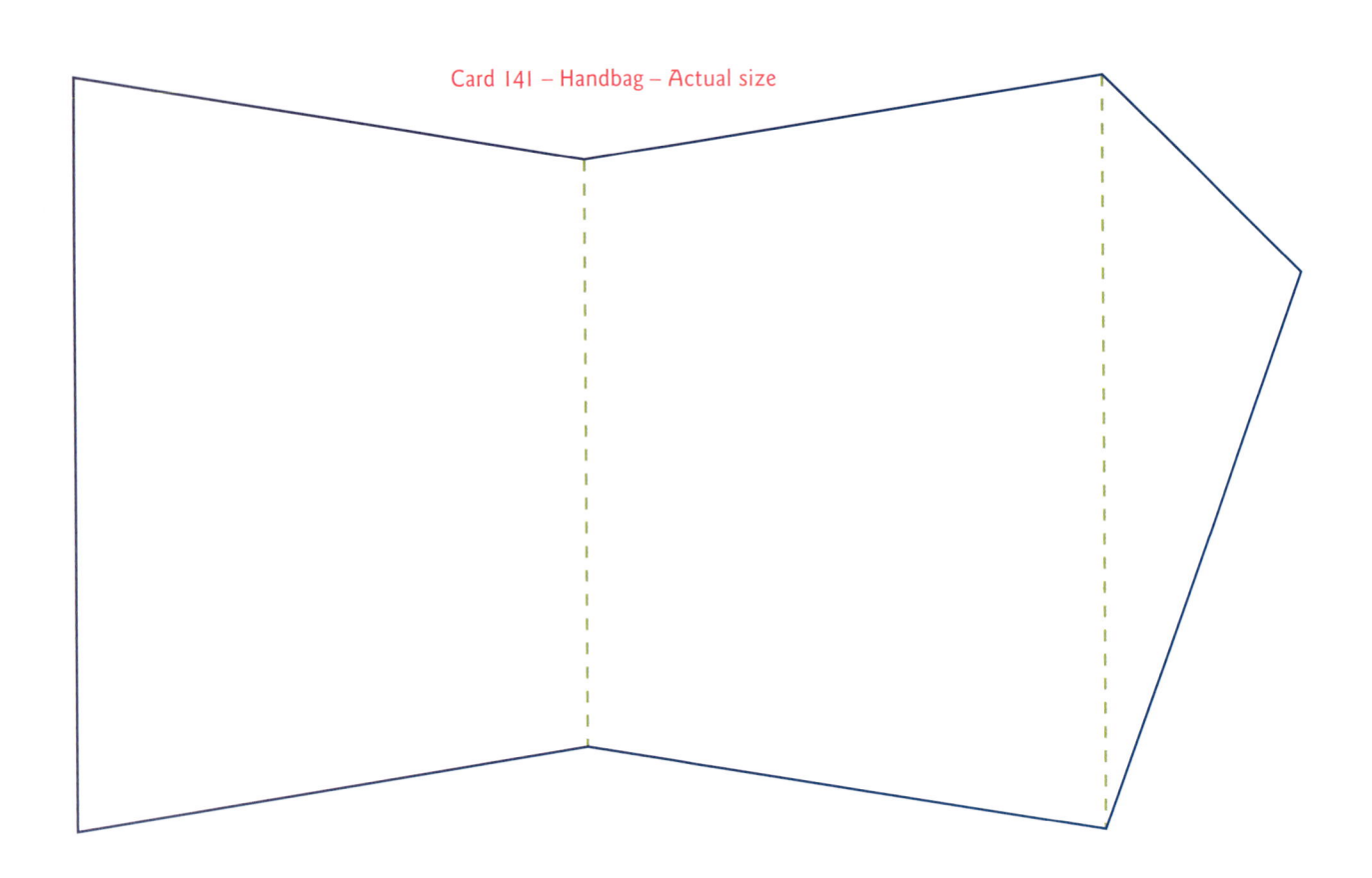

Card 142 – Christmas Tree
– Actual size

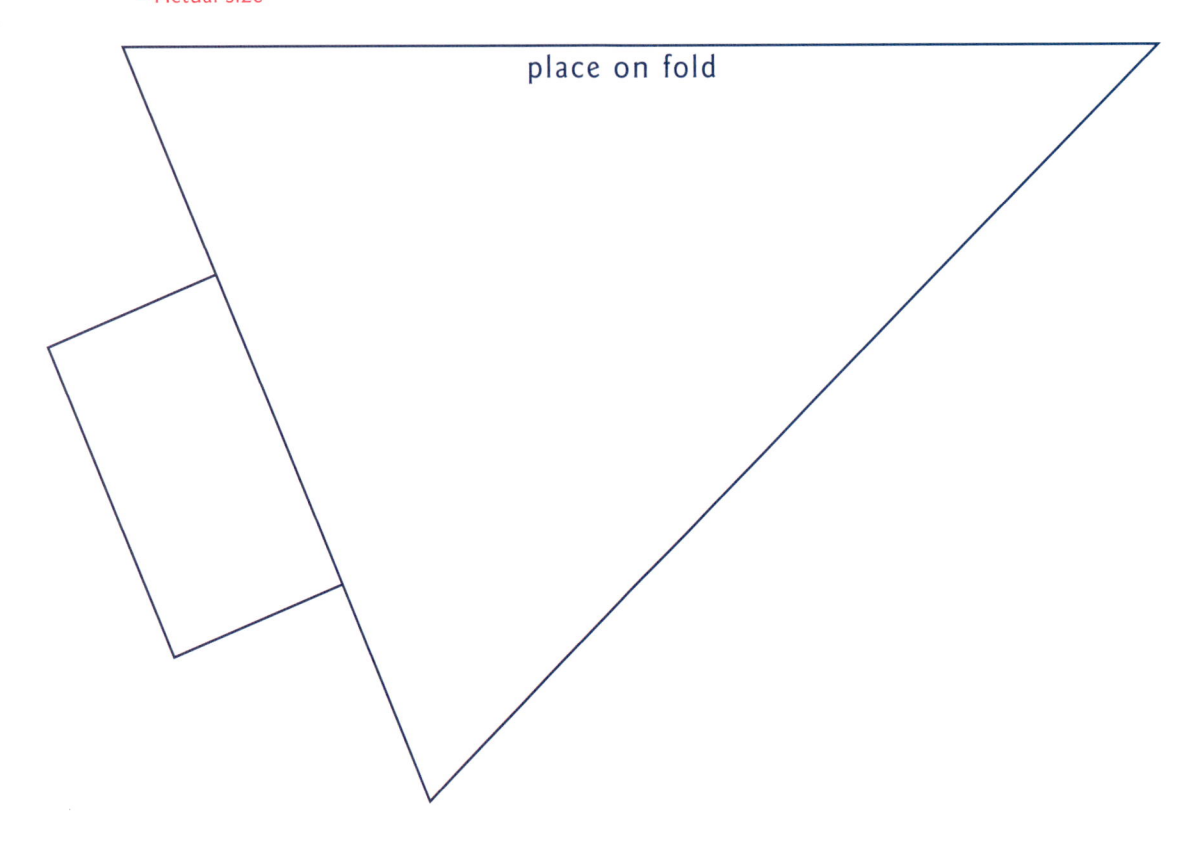

place on fold

110

Card 143 – JR's Wallet – Actual size

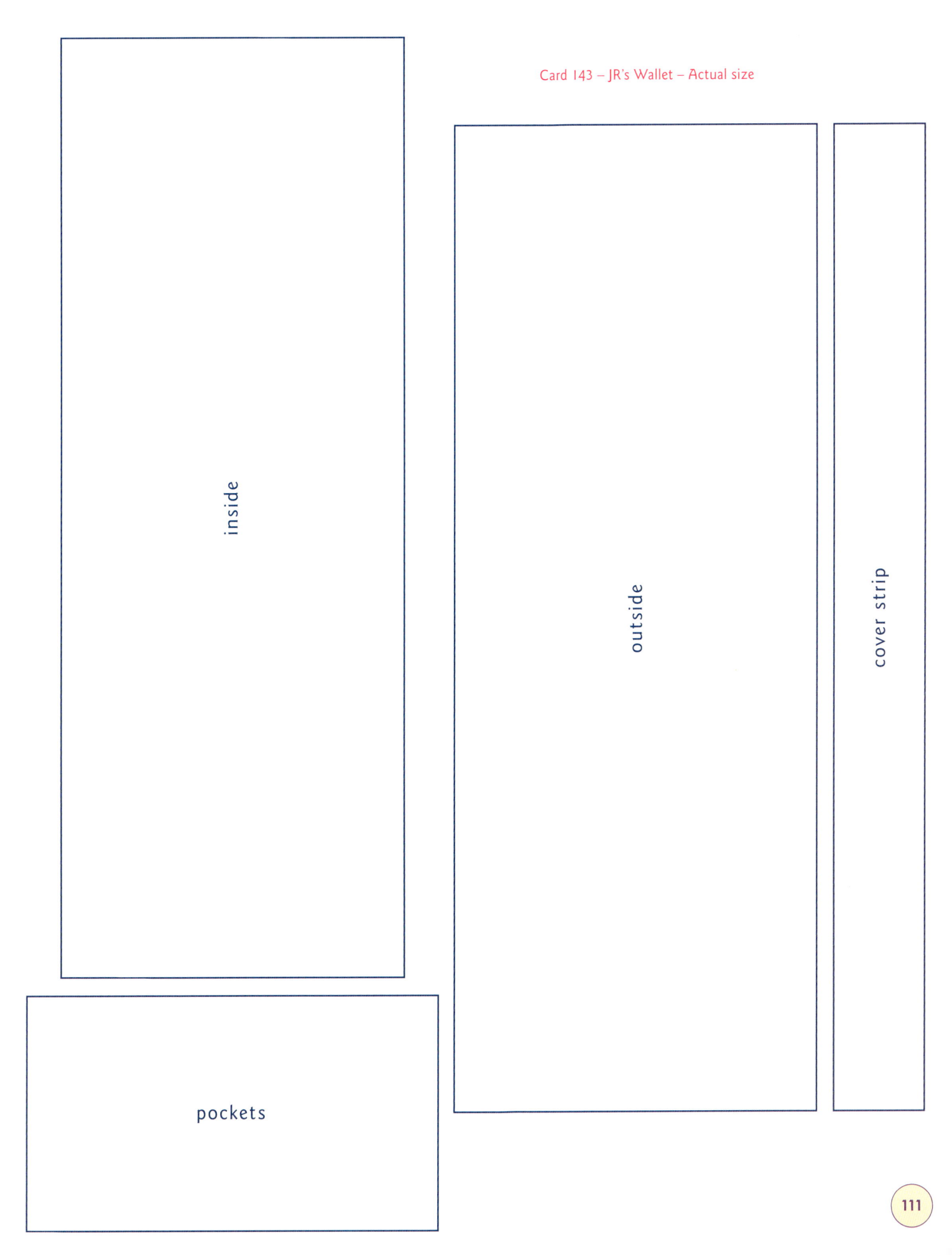

inside

outside

cover strip

pockets

Card 144 – New Home – Actual size

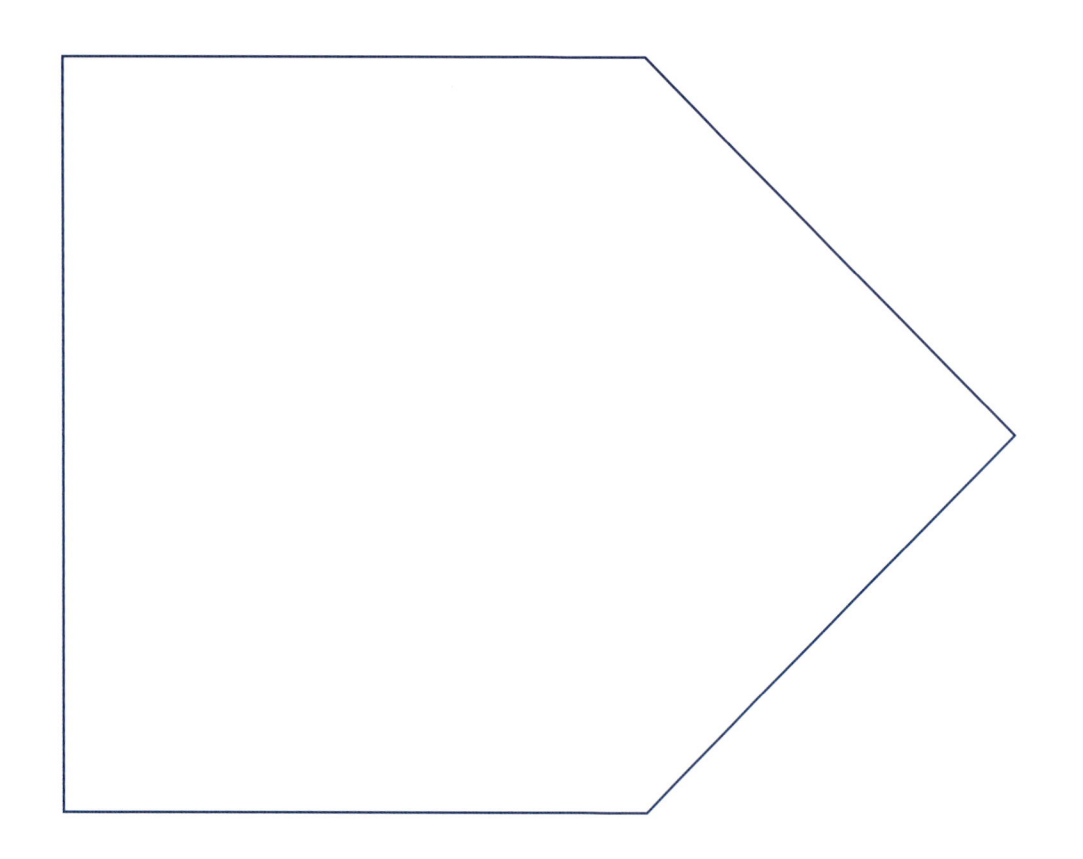

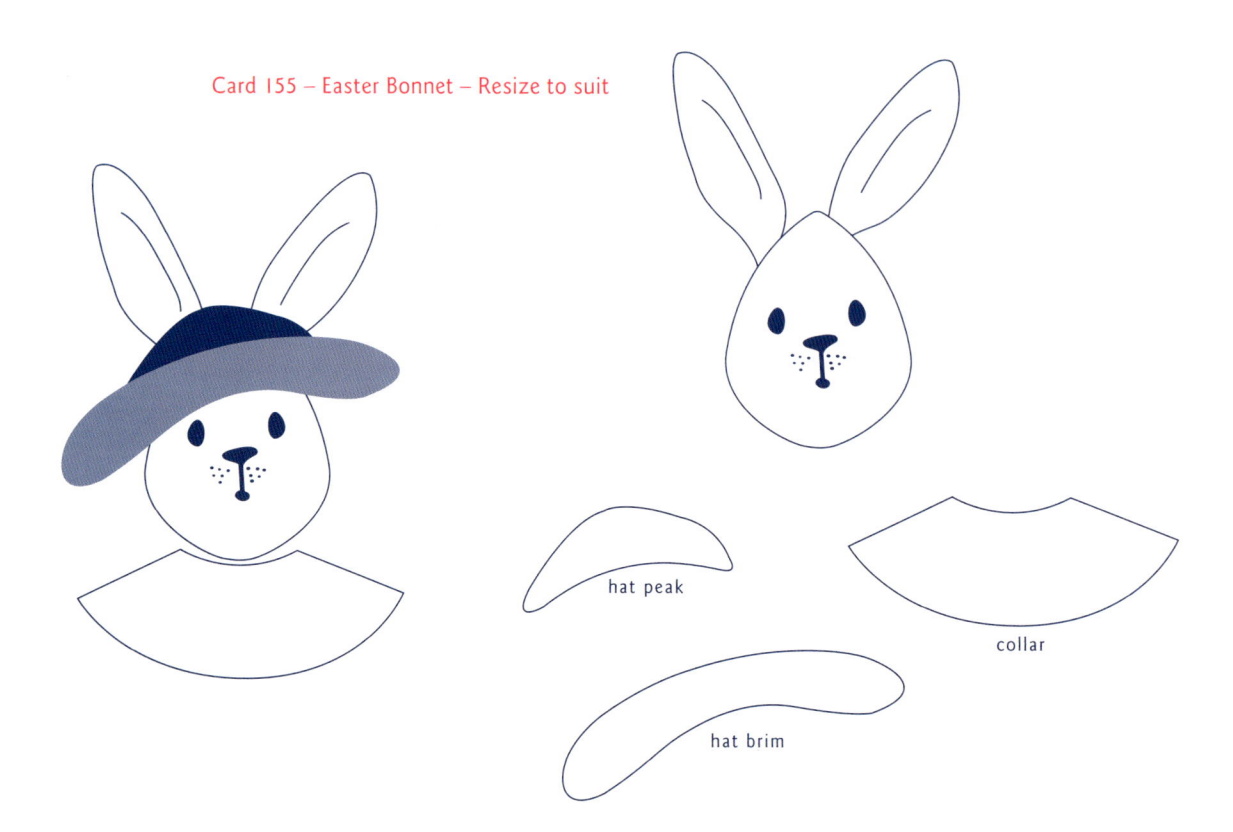

Card 155 – Easter Bonnet – Resize to suit

hat peak

hat brim

collar

112

Card 166 Beaded Flower – Stitching Guide – Resize to suit

place on centre of cardstock

A
B
C

Card 175 – Season's Greetings – Alternative diagram using one 420mm sheet of cardstock

140

90

mountain fold

90

valley fold

70

mountain fold

70

valley fold

50

mountain fold

50

420

Card 177 – Rayna's flower pot – Actual size

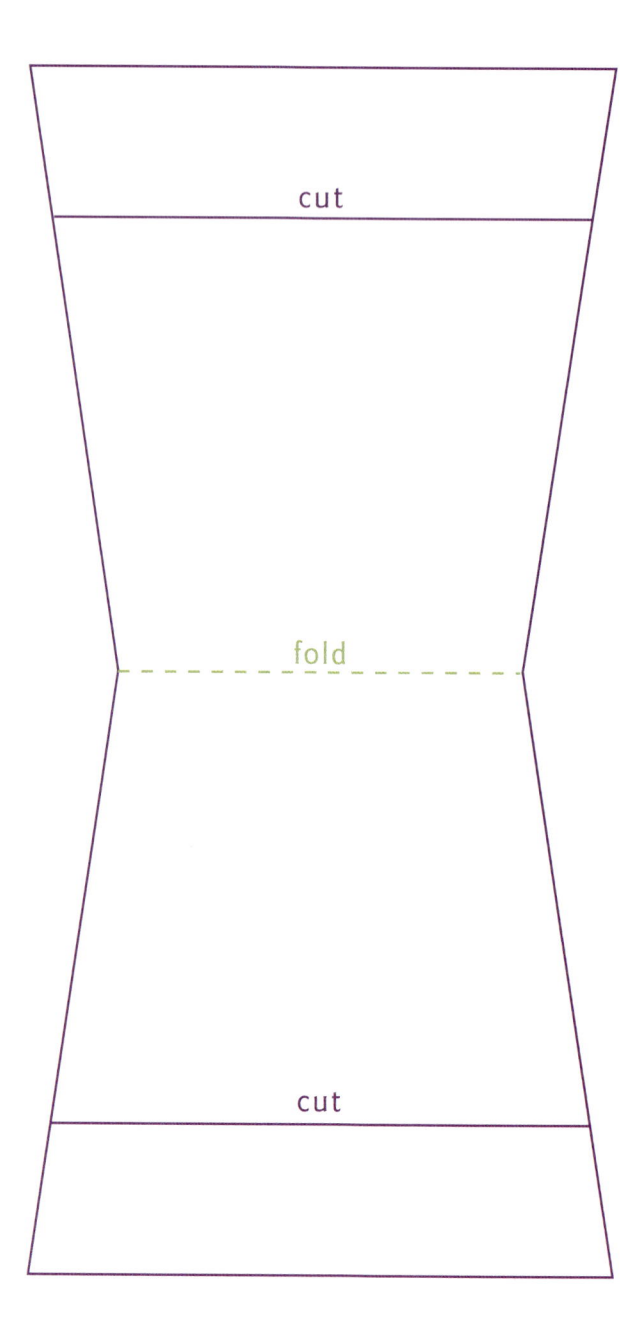

cut

fold

cut

Notes